ALSO BY JEANNE S. SILVERS:

Two Lumps of Clay in the Potter's House

The Life and Times of Jack and Becky Ryan

SOMEBODY FORGOT TO TELL THE KIDS

One Grandmother's Plea to the Church in America

JEANNE S. SILVERS

iUniverse LLC
Bloomington

SOMEBODY FORGOT TO TELL THE KIDS
ONE GRANDMOTHER'S PLEA TO THE CHURCH IN AMERICA

Scripture references are drawn from the King James Version or the New King James Version unless otherwise specifically noted.

Scripture references taken from the New King James Version. © 1982 by Thomas Nelson, Inc. Used by permission. All rights reserved.

Noted Scripture taken from The Message, Copyright © 1993, 1994, 1995, 1996, 2000, 2001, 2002. Used by permission of NavPress Publishing Group

iUniverse books may be ordered through booksellers or by contacting:

iUniverse LLC
1663 Liberty Drive
Bloomington, IN 47403
www.iuniverse.com
1-800-Authors (1-800-288-4677)

ISBN: 978-1-4917-1916-9 (sc)
ISBN: 978-1-4917-1917-6 (e)

Library of Congress Control Number: 2013923167

Printed in the United States of America.

iUniverse rev. date: 12/30/2013

CONTENTS

CHAPTER 12

CONCLUSION

ABOUT THE AUTHOR

NOTES

BIBLIOGRAPHY

PREFACE

Once I was young and now I am old…er. Someday I will be with Him where He is but not yet, not for a very long time I think. This age, this stage of life has caused me to reflect, to examine the world around me, to consider the future of this precious nation that I will leave as a heritage to future generations for every American bears a responsibility for that legacy. That charge is magnified for those of us who are true Christians. The weight of our charge is far, far greater than that of any other citizen.

And so I wonder. I wonder about my children, the generation now at the helm of our nation. I ponder the plight of my grandchildren as they march bravely into the workplace and through the halls of academia, fully prepared to grab the world by the throat until it surrenders to their will. And now I am a great-grandmother and I find that my attempts to envision the distant future world of that generation sputter and fail miserably. Who can even dream of the society they will create? I consider the changes that have exploded onto the scene in my own short lifetime and I struggle to imagine what America will look like when these young people are, say, fifty or sixty.

During the past twenty-one years I have been privileged to work alongside some truly great pastors and leaders within local churches in America, and I quickly discovered that there is one theme of prayer which is common to them all: the raging need for spiritual revival in America. It is this one shared issue that evokes depths of unmatched passion on the part of these wonderful church leaders. Let a prayer meeting turn to that particular petition and hearts beat a little faster and voices begin to lift a little higher in faith reaching out to the only One who could respond, for revival is His to give and somewhere deep in your spirit you sense that it pleases the Lord, that He agrees with your petition. And yet we wait. And our nation continues to suffer, and we feel helpless to bring healing to a broken land.

Past pondering is okay for a time and contemplative reflection can be beneficial, but change demands action. The church in America can no longer afford to sit by the roadway listening to the lies of hopelessness issuing forth from the mouth of the enemy of God; we must take another look at the chains with which we seem to be bound for they are nothing more than a lie, a clever deception.

It is that inevitability of yet uncharted tomorrows that brings about this writing. The future of our children, our grandchildren, and our great-grandchildren rests squarely upon our shoulders.

INTRODUCTION

Technology is not my forte. My friends are convinced that if it were possible I would probably walk around with a rotary phone stuck in my pocket, sans the interminable cell phone. I am much more comfortable with a good pen and a newly purchased pad of white lined paper than I am with cold, dreary computers. Nonetheless, here I sit facing a blank monitor screen wondering how to begin this exhortation. I suppose it is a given that I will be doing all the talking, but this particular journey is one that we must take together stopping occasionally to examine themes upon which we may or may not agree.

Maybe we should begin by clearly stating what this book is *not*.

- It is *not* about the sins of our society. I heard a great Sunday School teacher once say that we should not invest our energy in worrying about what the world is doing. They are just busy doing what the world does which is sin, and they are doing a mighty fine job of it I might add.
- It is *not* about how corrupt our nation has become. Any nation which shuns identification with Christ rushes headlong to an ill-fated destiny, surrendering itself to ever-deepening immorality and corruption.
- It is *not* about the span of the depravity assaulting our minds wherever we go. Let the world be the world and let the church be the church.

- It certainly is *not* about politics. It is the Lord who establishes kings and rulers.[1]

A light has begun to pierce the fog of disquiet and restlessness within the body of Christ in America, a light revealing intense and fervent longing for something real, something genuine. That beam of hope is making its way into Sunday morning pulpits; it is becoming a part of the everyday prayer life of true believers. The prayers and supplications of the saints have been heard and the responsive hand of God is moving and probing, searching for that remnant of people who are willing to pay the price for a breaking forth of His manifest presence.

Oh sure, brief, insulated occasions of spiritual revival (mercy drops, if you will) have emerged across our nation in recent decades, and for that we give Him praise, but what we are sensing now is different; we are ready for abundant showers. God is stirring up the church across America, causing us to become dissatisfied with the cold mediocrity of religion. That stirring you sense in your spirit is none other than the church of the living God, alive and well. The time is right for her to rise out of the fog of passivity and emerge as the tenderhearted and loving body of Christ, beautiful and splendid, with arms open wide to a population under siege.

My challenge then is to articulate exactly what this book *is* to become, and I think it can best be described as a handbook of exhortations centered upon unraveling the following conundrum:

IS THE CHURCH IN AMERICA LARGELY INEFFECTIVE TODAY BECAUSE OF THE DEPRAVED STATE OF OUR SOCIETY?

OR IS OUR SOCIETY IN THAT CORRUPT STATE BECAUSE THE CHURCH IS LARGELY INEFFECTIVE?

Home economics class in junior high school was nothing short of a nightmare for me. Cooking class was not so bad but sewing was a whole other story. I actually invented the high-low hemline that is so popular in today's fashions. Mrs. Chambers, may she rest in peace, made me rip out more seams than you can even imagine and so I speak with some authority on the topic of unraveling threads, which is precisely what we will attempt to do in order to solve the mystery of our puzzler. What thread comes first? Objectivity may the greatest hindrance to unbiased survey since self-examination can be pretty prickly; either we tend to see ourselves as faultless or we take upon ourselves guilt and condemnation. The former is woefully flawed and the latter is in complete contradiction to the Word of God, and so our goal will be to try to land somewhere in the middle with reflections of balance, striving to see ourselves as God sees us and not as we perceive ourselves.

If we take our stance on a high plane where we can look objectively at the church in America today, it truly is a thing of perfected beauty...... at first glance. Our buildings are contemporary and visually striking along the streets of our cities and the side roads of rural life. The pews are ergonomically pleasing, the lighting is restfully pleasant to the eye, and the temperature is computer-controlled to keep us green-conscious and wonderfully comfy at the same time. The music in its presentation is probably as good or better than it has ever been, and our technology is state of the art, and yet under the revealing light of the Word of God our local assemblies find themselves sorely lacking in many ways, not because God failed to equip but because we have attempted to disguise ourselves in order to be more palatable to the society around us.

In the early 1800's, a certain Cherokee Chief named Yonaguska had given a group of missionaries permission to teach Cherokee children to read and write, using the Holy Bible as a textbook. However, he insisted that he must hear the teachings first before they could be introduced to the young ones. "After listening, he very seriously remarked, 'Well, it seems to be a good book, but it is strange that the white people are not better after having it so long.'"[2]

Well might the same statement be made of the church in America today. We have in our possession all that we need to become *"like a tree planted by the rivers of water, that brings forth its fruit in its season...,"*[3] bringing light and hope to a people desperate for answers and yet we find ourselves in a state of apparent paralysis.

So how do we get there? How do we break the hold of our perceived helplessness? A great pastor once pointed out to me that the federal housing complex in his city was surrounded by a high security fence topped by a foot-high barbed wire crown. This government office existed for the sole purpose of serving the poor, but the thorny crest of the fence was slanted outward to ward off the very people for whom it existed. Sadly, that is remarkably like any self-absorbed local church.

Leaders of our individual assemblies almost universally express disenchantment with their outreach efforts, always searching for more effective means, probing the pulse of the surrounding culture to find that vulnerable opening. Amid occasional reports of effective community outreach our overall efforts, well thought out and developed though they might be, have been doomed to failure. The sting of these letdowns has prompted many pastors to content themselves with busy work inside the four walls, leaving the world to fend for itself.

It is actually a healthy thing, this heartbreaking disappointment, for if there were not hope there would be no disappointment. In recent years the following Scripture has become one of the most widely known and quoted verses of the Bible:

> *Jeremiah 29:11, "[11]For I know the thoughts that I think toward you, says the Lord, thoughts of peace and not of evil, to give you a future and a hope."*

The idea that God has a destiny and a plan for each of us is almost incomprehensible in its fullest scope, and yet it is true because the Bible says it is. Our thought process might go something like this: It was He who made a way of salvation through the atoning sacrifice in Christ; it was He *"who also has sealed us and given us the Spirit in our hearts as a guarantee"*[4]*; and it was He who "endued with power from on high"*[5] in order that we might be witnesses to every nation including our own. Having made such powerful provision, would He now gain some inexplicable satisfaction by thwarting our effectiveness? Has He looked away, neglecting to see our plans come to naught time after time? As the apostle Paul might have said: God forbid! His Word, His justice, His righteousness, His character, His omniscience all demand a resounding, "NO!" We are the apple of His eye, sheltered under His wing[6]. His plan unfolds before us and He takes great satisfaction when we gain victories, but there is another aspect of God's character that we absolutely must remember: He offends His Word for no man.

Let it be crystal clear that this is *not* an indictment of the church in America! Au contraire! Pastors, pastoral staff, elders, deacons, teachers, and workers continually search for ways to reach outside the house of God to the lost, only to find that most of their time is occupied keeping their congregation *inside* the house of God in their proper place of worship and service. Discouragement – especially long-term discouragement – can cause these great men and women of God to grow weary and weariness can result in lowered expectations.

Reaping a spiritual harvest in America today is akin to attempting to raise crops of corn and wheat in the middle of a shifting desert, but our great pastors and our leaders, undaunted and courageous, just keep at it and keep at it. Maybe a new structure. Maybe a new leader here or there. Maybe new equipment. Maybe dynamic special speakers. Maybe…

Let me encourage you today, dear men and women of God, your unrelenting efforts have not gone unnoticed by the Lord. It is, after all, the Holy Spirit who moves upon us to keep trying, to keep pursuing, to press on. He sees our efforts, the strain and the drain and He waits patiently for us to realize that all we have to do is ask and believe.

Zechariah 4:6, "⁶Then he answered and spoke unto me, saying, This is the word of the LORD unto Zerubbabel, saying, Not by might, nor by power, but by my spirit, saith the LORD of hosts."

A number of years ago I heard a highly respected gentleman speak before a conglomeration of civic leaders in a major city, addressing in particular some of the problems which plague our inner cities. The well-formulated and passionately presented lecture was entitled, "The Nation Which Hates Its Children." The title says it all, doesn't it? The content pierced the heart of any willing listener. As an example, just two days prior to this writing the news carried a story of the arrest of a sixty-one year old man who worked as a teacher in an elementary school. He had been charged with twenty-three counts of criminal confinement and various other charges based upon having taken little children (one at a time over an extended period) into a remote room in the school where he bound them hand and foot, gagged them, and loosed upon them containers of live cockroaches. Once the child responded in the horrific fear that can only be felt and expressed by a child they were then forced to ingest his bodily fluids, after which the child was released to return to class, threatened with a repeat if they told anyone. At least twenty-three times this happened. How can this happen in what we blissfully know as the greatest nation on earth? How did we become so hardened, so incredibly insensible? How long

In America:

- In 2006 U. S. Attorneys handled 82.8% more child pornography cases than they had in 1994.
- There was a 230% increase in the number of documented complaints of online enticement of children from 2004 to 2008.
- As of June 2013, National Center for Missing and Exploited Children has reviewed and analyzed more than 90 million child pornography images since its creation in 2002.

National Center for Missing and Exploited Children
www.missingkids.com/NCMEC

can a nation survive when it hates its own children? The maladies of our society are not confined to despicable acts toward our children, but they are a major indicator of just how far we have fallen.

I am tempted at this point to resort to statistics and readily available data on the social ills of America at large to substantiate the adjectives "corrupt" and "depraved." After all, I reasoned, if we expect to discuss solutions should we not first clearly state the problem? I determined however that one half-hour session of the evening news rendered that unnecessary. You already know the state of our society so we will settle for some strategically placed reminders. While experts attempt to explain away the ills of society from their various viewpoints, the evidence, when contrasted with the word of God, is undeniable. Something has gone horribly wrong in America and the church must take steps to reflect its true identity: that of the Body of Christ.

The following oft quoted Scripture places the blame squarely where it belongs:

> 2nd *Chronicles 7:14, "^{14}If My people who are called by My name will humble themselves, and pray and seek My face, and turn from their wicked ways, then I will hear from heaven, and will forgive their sin and heal their land."*

C. S. Lewis presented us with an intensely profound thought (as only Lewis can) in his "Out of the Silent Planet" space trilogy which went something like this: Once you have tasted of the good things of the Lord (that other, spiritual world) there's no going back. You who have seen and known the majesty, the overwhelming beauty, and the matchless grace of God simply cannot revert to the indifferent existence you knew before because you have been forever changed by His presence.

> 2nd *Corinthians 5:17, "^{17}Therefore, if anyone is in Christ, he is a new creation; old things have passed away; behold, all things have become new."*

That is a spectacular concept whose full ramifications are probably well beyond our ability to comprehend. What we *do* know is that the old things of the old life passed away at that point in time and all things became new, a process which continues until we

In 2009 an estimated 1,770 children died from abuse in the U. S. with the age group of newborn to one year having the highest rate of victimization.

U. S. Department of
Health and Human Services
www.childwelfare.gov.can.statistics

leave this world as we are continuously being conformed to the image of Christ Himself. We are most apt to apply that Scripture to the Holy Spirit's molding of our character and spiritual walk, but must we not also apply it to how He prompts us to relate to those who are without Christ and therefore without hope?

Before you heard His heart beat and saw the immeasurable love in His eyes there was no compulsion to reach those around you, but alas, all things have now become new. Now you see those people through His eyes and the landscape has changed. Now you look around and you see families falling apart, a destruction of the most elementary of societal units created at the hands of God in the Garden of Eden and your heart cries out but your hands seem to be tied. Now the vacant stare of confused children haunts you and your heart breaks but to what end? The hungry (spiritually *and* physically) are at every turn but what is a person (or in this case a local church) to do? The needs have overwhelmed us to such a degree that our effort to reach out resembles a game of blind man's bluff.

Living in a state of indifference toward the society around you is no longer an option for you. The Apostle Paul described himself this way:

Ephesians 3:1, "For this reason I, Paul, the prisoner of
Christ Jesus for you Gentiles…"

In Romans 11:13, Paul referred to himself as the apostle of the Gentiles. He had been appointed of God to preach the gospel to the Gentiles, and so deep was that conviction that he described himself in Ephesians 3:1 as the *prisoner* of Christ Jesus on behalf of those Gentiles. Paul never gave his persecutors credit for his stints in the prisons or the hand of brutal torment; instead, he acknowledged the Lordship of Jesus Christ and therefore became a sort of prisoner of his hope.

In like manner the church is a prisoner of that hope on behalf of all men everywhere. In fact, Paul put an even more penetrating light on the role of every Christian:

> Romans 1:14-15, "*14I am a debtor both to Greeks and to barbarians, both to wise and to unwise. 15So, as much as is in me, I am ready to preach the gospel to you who are in Rome also.*"

Verse 15 brings up the image of an Indiana Jones-style pose, Paul holding his nose and posturing himself to jump off a cliff into a

| 16,272 |
| The number of forcible rapes. |
| *U. S. Census Bureau* |
| *Statistical Abstract of the U. S.: 2012* |

raging torrent below. Persecution followed him everywhere he went not because he was Paul but because he preached the gospel of Jesus Christ and he did so without shame or fear of repercussion. When we read the words "*as much as is in me*" we get a hint that Paul knew further persecution was likely inevitable and yet onward he marched. Likewise today the body of Christ owes a debt of love to a nation crying out for relief. That dissatisfaction that you experience daily, that drive which propels you along the way in the work of the ministry is simply the Holy Spirit leading you on to reach for the stars and since it is He who gives that vision then it is He who will help you realize your dreams.

Does that mean that we scrap everything we are doing today in the church? Of course not. We believers have historically been guilty of discovering some beautiful revealed truth or some key that we perceive might open the doors to a demonstration of the power of God in our midst, only to emphasize that new area of truth so strenuously that we become unbalanced in many *other* truths, neglecting areas which are equally important. We become unbalanced. We have seen this cycle play out in areas such as positive confession, physical healing, end times, intellectual teachings, and community praise and worship. Each of these areas is based upon Bible truths, each has contributed enormously to the life and health of believers, and each should continue to be taught until the day the Lord returns. We should celebrate these truths, teach these truths, and observe these truths. However, it is incumbent upon the church today to amass a balance of church life which produces healthy, vibrant, peaceable, content, and *reproductive* sheep.

> "You never change things by fighting the existing reality. To change something, build a new model that makes the existing model obsolete."[7]

While the above statement was made within a very secular context the thought can be beneficial to us as Christians as well. Perhaps the church in America today is not the power wielding body that we ought to be but change cannot and will not come by seeking to point the finger at this church or that church or this person or that person. Instead, change will come when we cease busyness and seek after the Lord. Period. Remember our commission in 2nd Chronicles?

Where do we begin such a monumental examination? Where we are today. Where do we set up base camp? In the Bible, the only one source for absolute truth, the place where every fruitful search for wisdom begins. Our study will be based upon the story of Elijah as he witnessed the very fire of the Lord fall upon the altar consuming the burnt sacrifice and the wood and the stones and the dust and even the water in the trench. However, the display of power in the now famous story of Elijah did not begin with the responsive fire of the Lord. The overwhelming display of God's power was assured as Elijah methodically and watchfully made preparation.

When the antics of the prophets of Baal had failed to produce even one scrap of evidence of their god, Elijah stepped up to the plate, full of faith in the God of Israel:

> *1ˢᵗ Kings 18:30, "³⁰Then Elijah said to all the people, 'Come near to me.' So all the people came near to him. And he repaired the altar of the Lord that was broken down."*

This is not intended to be an all-inclusive, comprehensive study of that day on Mount Carmel for that would distract us from our questions. We will instead focus primarily on this one verse and particularly the last portion of that verse, *"and he repaired the altar of the Lord that was broken down."*

> In 2009 roughly 1.1 million children or 1.5% of all children in America lived in the home of a parent who divorced the previous year.
>
> *U. S. Census Bureau*
> *Statistical Abstract of the U.S.: 2012*

The very word "altar" rightly brings a sense of foreboding since it literally means, "a place of slaughter." Altars were most often built as exactly that (a place of slaughter) and occasionally they were built as a memorial, but every altar built as a tribute to Jehovah God spoke forward through time to the day of that final altar, the cross of Calvary.

> *John 8:56-58, "⁵⁶Your father Abraham rejoiced to see My day, and he saw it and was glad.' ⁵⁷Then the Jews said to Him, 'You are not yet fifty years old, and have You seen Abraham?' ⁵⁸Jesus said to them, 'Most assuredly, I say to you, before Abraham was, I AM.'"*

There is something in the human psyche which is repulsed by the shedding of blood, and in fact many have removed all reference to the shed blood of Christ, both in their music and in their teaching. This exhortation is not directed to such as would reject the heavenly, but bloody, sacrifice of the cross for they have made their choice; instead, it is intended to exhort and edify those who desire with all their hearts to be ambassadors for Christ.

Ahab reigned upon the throne of the northern kingdom of Israel in the day of Elijah. That particular throne apparently was the size of a modern-day loveseat because on the cushion beside Ahab sat the powerful and cruel Jezebel.

> 1ˢᵗ *Kings 16:31-33, "³¹And it came to pass, as though it had been a trivial thing for him to walk in the sins of Jeroboam, the son of neighbor Nebat, that he took as his wife Jezebel the daughter of Ethbaal, King of the Sidonians; and he went and served Baal and worshipped him. ³²Then he set up an altar for Baal in the Temple of Baal, which he had built in Samaria. ³³And Ahab made a wooden image. Ahab did more to provoke the Lord God of Israel to anger than all the kings of Israel who were before him."*

It is interesting to note that as bad as it had been for Ahab to participate in the sins of Jeroboam, his transgression in taking Jezebel as his wife was far more tragic. In the days leading up to the notable scene on Mount Carmel, Jezebel had undertaken to obliterate all vestige of the

Over 200 babies under one year of age were murdered in the U. S. in 2009.

Slightly over 300 between the ages of 1 to 4 were murdered.

Those over 70: 429

U. S. Census Bureau
Statistical Abstract of the U.S. 2012

days of the worship of the one true God of Israel. This delusional woman was actually convinced that she could wipe all memory of Jehovah God off the face of the earth. Her attack was far-reaching; however, her main stratagem was twofold: to destroy the prophets of God and to tear down the altars used in His worship for without the altar of sacrifice there was no worship. In sharp contrast to the days of Jezebel, the enemy of God can no longer destroy the altar:

> *Hebrews 10:8-10, "*^{8}*Previously saying, 'Sacrifice and offering, burnt offerings, and offerings for sin You did not desire, nor had pleasure in them' (which are offered according to the law),* ^{9}*then He said, 'Behold I have come to do Your will, O God.' He takes away the first that He may establish the second.* ^{10}*By that will we have been sanctified through the offering of the body of Jesus Christ once for all."*

Once for all. Complete. A finished work. Satan's only remaining option of attack, therefore, is to prevent you and me from letting our *"light so shine before men, that they may see your good works and glorify your Father in heaven."*[8] That has always been the thrust of God's plan, to show forth His goodness and His grace to His people as an irresistible invitation to all men, but mankind has never been able to sustain that Divine reflection long enough for it to entice. Let us resolve to take a page from Paul's life and refuse to give satan more credit than he deserves. We all agree that he has a modicum of power in this world, measured by the yardstick of our own willingness to heed his lies. However, the quagmire in which the church is bogged seems to be of our own making in many respects.

> *1st Kings 18:30, "*^{30}*Then Elijah said to all the people, 'Come near to me.' So all the people came near to him. And he repaired the altar of the Lord that was broken down."*

The Bible does not specifically give Jezebel credit for having torn down this particular altar. It appears as though the altar on Mount Carmel had deteriorated through decay and neglect on the part of the people of Israel. Who can blame them? That Jezebel was one scary woman and she had an endless array of cruel executioners to carry out her decrees. That being the case, it is likely that this altar did not end up in its deteriorated state overnight, but that it wore down over a period of time, one compromise at a time, until it finally became no more than a common pile of rocks. As God looked down upon Mount Carmel that day His eye was not upon the prophets of Baal for He had no respect for them and their counterfeit worship, but upon His own people who stood gathered around that pile of stones like shamefaced children. As wretched and pitiful as they had become, they represented a nation chosen by God to be known by His name and it was He who knew what had led each man to that place of idolatry and perversion and it was He who knew how to draw them back. In like manner, the New Testament church in America, in spite of having compromised on some of the basic tenets of the faith, is a part of God's *"holy nation"*[9] known by His name. He knows precisely how to draw us back to being salt and light to our land.

> An average of nearly five children die in America every day from abuse and/or neglect.
>
> *Every Child Matters*
> *http://everychildmatters.org*

Our man, Elijah, very deliberately began to set things in order for an indisputable, powerful visual demonstration that there was but one true God….. and His name was not Baal. There in the sight of all the people Elijah began to repair the altar one stone at a time until all twelve stones were in place, knowing full well that God does not deviate from His declared word for any man, and then having completed his task, he dedicated it to the name of the Lord.

I am sure that you know the end of the story quite well. If perchance you do not then you should stop now and read it for yourself in 1ˢᵗ Kings 18:30–39. (BTW, God wins the event!)

As the altar of Elijah was constructed of twelve stones according to the number of the tribes of the sons of Jacob, we will divide our study into twelve general areas common to the life of every believer and every assembly within the local church. It is probable that each person who reads and considers these twelve areas will view them quite differently and that is okay so long as the Word is not offended. This is not an effort at some lofty ecumenical rhapsody, but rather an exhortation to all true believers to shed the cloak of arrogant religion and rise to reflect His desire for us:

> *Ephesians 5:25-27, "²⁵Husbands, love your wives, just as Christ also loved the church and gave Himself for her, ²⁶that He might sanctify and cleanse her with the washing of water by the word, ²⁷that He might present her to Himself a glorious church, not having spot or wrinkle or any such thing, but that she should be holy and without blemish."*

May we, having thoroughly and objectively examined ourselves, witness the marvelous power of the Lord, the very same unchangeable, eternally existent God worshipped by Elijah. May the society in which we live begin to see us, the body of Christ, as He intended us to be: full of love, joy, peace, longsuffering, gentleness, goodness, faith, meekness, and self-control.

CHAPTER 1

A RETROSPECT

The little room was packed on that hot summer night. The crowd leaned forward as one, almost as if by mutual consent, the old wooden pews groaning under the shifting weight. Small children slept on rough wooden floors on makeshift pallets of feather pillows and hand stitched quilts, blissfully unaware of all that went on around them.

Windows were thrown open to catch what night time breeze might find its way in, but that was unlikely on that muggy, sticky night, the kind of night when you pray for cool rain. The only breeze to be found in that little church came from tattered cardboard fans wobbling precariously on scalloped wooden sticks.

And yet no one noticed the crowd or the hard pews or the stifling heat because their attention was riveted on the man of God as he opened up the Bible and began to speak. The message was both simply profound and profoundly simple: Jesus, the only begotten Son of God who came to die on a manmade cross, shedding His blood so that no one need perish. Each man, each woman and each child under the sound of his voice heard their own story that night because the Spirit of the Lord was so prevailing. Truth from the Word of God began its work of slowly peeling away the layers of sham and pretense that religion brings, revealing the beauty of grace.

It was a sight to behold. Sweat began to bead up on the face of the old preacher and slowly found its way onto the shoulders of what had once been a finely starched and hot-ironed white shirt. His tie had already found its way across the room, snaked unceremoniously across the old piano bench.

Here and there tears ran down the cheeks of the Christians in that room as conviction and forgiveness flowed freely. It was easy to spot the folks who had never met Jesus. Their body language gave them away, as they shifted anxiously first this way and then that, their troubled thoughts clearly written on their faces. Why had they come that night? What was it which had drawn them through the doors? How did the preacher know all about him, his loneliness and despair, his yearning for love? He was a failure in the eyes of the world, his sin black as the starless night. How could the death of that one lone man at Calvary possibly change all that? That was the *natural* man talking. The *spirit* man wanted just one thing: to touch Jesus.

As the message reached its thundering crescendo, the little choir began to sing:

> *Almost persuaded now to believe;*
> *Almost persuaded Christ to receive;*
> *Seems now some soul to say,*
> *Go, Sprit, go Thy way,*
> *Some more convenient day*
> *On Thee I'll call.*[10]

There was not a trained voice among them, but when they lifted up their voices in four-part harmony, I declare it sounded like the angels of heaven chimed in. There was a pleading in the song and in their voices, an unashamed passion for the ones that Jesus loved so much.

The old wooden altar would not stand empty for long. It had played host to generations of the worst of sinners seeking forgiveness; to mothers and fathers heartbroken over wayward children and to husbands and wives crying out in despair over shattered marriages; to lonely people searching for a Divine Friend and to men and women enslaved by sin.

And so they sang.

Almost persuaded, come, come today;
Almost persuaded, turn not away;
Jesus invites you here,
Angels are lingering near,
Prayers rise from hearts so dear,
O wanderer, come.

Come on, wanderer, come on. The atmosphere crackled with anticipation as people began to move toward the old wooden altar, kneeling here and there in the same grooves worn by the kneeling form of previous generations as they had taken refuge there. Each person who knelt there that night needed something different from Jesus and no one went away disappointed. No one ever leaves the presence of Jesus disappointed.

But not everyone responded. Not everyone gravitated toward Jesus. There was a tumultuous battle going on the in that room. Saints were weeping aloud, praying for lost sons and daughters and friends. All over the building the hands of the lost clutched the backs of pews fighting to resist Christ's redemptive call choosing to cling instead to an old, decayed life of sin. Here and there the hands unclenched and feet did the heart's bidding. But not everyone.

Almost persuaded, harvest is past!
Almost persuaded, doom comes at last!
Almost cannot avail;
Almost is but to fail!
Sad, sad, that bitter wail,
Almost....but lost.

The writer of this song penned these words after listening to a sermon based upon this thought: He who is almost persuaded is almost saved, but to be almost saved is to be entirely lost.

That is my recollection of that night as my memory reaches backward some sixty years. Some would describe this scene as Elmer Gantryesque, but they would be wrong. There was no theatrical manipulation that night, just a simple man given over to a mighty God. As the people had entered the refuge of that little church, they had left behind a venomous world and walked into an atmosphere of mutual love and acceptance. They had sung His praises, not by rote, but with passion and in unity in four-part harmony. The preacher had presented to them the Bible, not a set of principles *about* the Bible, mind you, but the Word of God itself. They had heard the unmitigated truth of heaven and hell and verbal road signs had been posted along the way, warning of the need for salvation. And then they heard of a thing called grace and the road map was complete.

What would I give to walk into a service like that once again! What happened? How did the simplicity of the gospel of Jesus Christ become so obscure, so shrouded in ethics and cold principles?

The answer is so simple as to defy belief: Somebody forgot to tell the kids.

CHAPTER 2

APPROACHING THE ALTAR

We stand now amongst that multitude on Mount Carmel. Feel the sunshine on your skin and breathe the stale atmosphere of the uneasy crowd; allow yourself to be jostled and nudged by those trying to get a better view. If you listen closely, you will hear the whispered conversations of the Jews who had been summoned that day. They had no idea what to expect, but when they saw the "*hairy man wearing a leather belt around his waist*"[11] they pretty much knew this was not going to be an ordinary day.

You go first, phony prophets.

The prophets of Baal were given first dibs in this contest and like a major-leaguer ready to step up to the plate in the bottom of the ninth, these boys began to call upon the name of Baal. Most likely they even called out his name, "Baal! Oh Baal! Answer our call, Baal!" This crying out continued from morning until noon, "O Baal, hear us! O Baal, answer us!" Perhaps Baal desired something a little more demonstrative in their plea? The men began to leap and dance around the altar and its sacrifice so carefully prepared in the name of Baal. Elijah tried to help them out (tongue in cheek of course) by suggesting that perhaps they might want to shout louder since Baal might be meditating or taking a call on his I-phone or he might have even gone on vacation or catnapping. Those pitiable men exhausted themselves in their attempts to trigger some responsive act by Baal, including cutting themselves until their own blood flowed. The Bible states clearly the end of that matter and I cannot outdo its wording: "....*there was no voice; no one answered, no one paid attention.*"[12] Well said, Lord.

Elijah did not miss a beat, but this was not an isolated go-out-on-a-limb kind of faith because the Lord had strategically equipped him for this moment long before coming to the mountain. It was only because Elijah had been willing to allow God to prepare him over a period of time that he could now step forward with the utmost faith and confidence. The first thing he did was to invite all Israel to be witnesses:

> *1ˢᵗ Kings 18:30,* "³⁰ *Then Elijah said to all the people, 'Come near to me.' So all the people came near to him, and he repaired the altar of the Lord that was broken down.*"

Why did Elijah specifically call the people of Israel to huddle so close to that dilapidated altar? Was the battle on Mount Carmel not designed to show forth the supreme authority and power of the God of Israel over this weak and unresponsive Baal? Should not Ahab and the false prophets have had the premium seats that day? The manifestation of Divine supremacy was certainly one of the goals of the showdown, but our God is not threatened by those who seek to bully Him into playground scuffles. We would do well to remember that in our daily walk. When He moves and shows forth His power and authority it is to reveal His omnipotence and sovereignty, drawing men to worship. When all was said and done, it turned out *not* to be a good day to be a false prophet for they were all summarily executed at Elijah's command.

So why did Elijah summon the people to come close to him? He was setting the stage for the people of God to observe the man of God as he called upon the power of God so that they could make a choice to serve their God. Do you remember Elijah's earlier question?

1ˢᵗ Kings 18:21b, "…..How long will you falter between two opinions? If the Lord is God, follow him; but if Baal, follow him."

Elijah's faith was front and center of this theatrical demonstration and, in fact, Elijah's faith must have been known far and wide because earlier in Chapter 18 we read Ahab's response when he finally came face to face with Elijah, *"Is that you, O troubler of Israel?"*[13] Ahab, arrogant and egomaniacal Ahab, was disinclined to bear any of the blame for the drought and subsequent starvation of the people under his rule. Like the people of Israel he had been faced with a choice long prior and he chose to worship the Baals (the very name meaning lord, possessor, or husband). Baal had become the object of his faith, and yet by his very own words Ahab testified to the supremacy of Elijah's God who had decreed a national crisis that his own god could not solve.

Romans 6:15-16, "¹⁵What then? Shall we sin because we are not under law but under grace? Certainly not! ¹⁶Do you not know that to whom you present yourselves slaves to obey, you are that one's slaves whom you obey, whether of sin leading to death, or of obedience leading to righteousness."

This principle was at work in Ahab, Jezebel, and the other worshipers of Baal. By virtue of their worship and blind obedience they had become enslaved to a conjured non-entity, relinquishing great power over their lives even to the point of self-torture and human sacrifice. This god was given honor and glory when crops and flocks and herds prospered and were plentiful and when they failed the people would engage in unbelievably heinous acts in an effort to gain approval of a nonexistent being. Say what you will about these worshipers of Baal, their faith was beyond reproach; but the exercise of faith on the part of man is only as powerful as the object of that faith and in Elijah's case the object of his worship, adoration, and lordship was the one true God with whom nothing is impossible.

Every Christian will have a Mount Carmel sometime.

The Lord manifested some quite incredible miracles during the life of Elijah, but it is this Mount Carmel scene that comes first to our mind. Pause for just a moment and ask yourself whether that is true for you. When the name of Elijah is spoken what comes to your mind? Is it the scene by the Brook Cherith where he was fed by ravens? How about the cake maker widow at Zarephath? Why the Lord even revived the soul of a boy and returned him to life at the hand of Elijah, but is that the one that comes to your mind? Probably not. We almost always associate the name of Elijah with the scene at Mount Carmel.

Why do you think that is? What is it about the story that intrigues us so much? The simple story which occupies only one part of one chapter of the Bible is resplendent with excitement and drama, a shoo-in for Hollywood kudos for the spectacular climax. Nonetheless, it seems that it is not the drama that draws us but the intriguing way that a simple man named Elijah had the courage to step out from among the crowd and put his faith on the block, something that many of us have felt led to do from time to time (admittedly on a lesser scale) but simply have not had the courage to respond.

I often recall the very first time I was called to the hospital as a minister of the gospel. A young seventeen year old boy had been taken to the emergency room by ambulance after sustaining life-threatening injuries in a pickup game of football. I remember driving to see him in a bit of a fog, knowing full well that the family would be under great distress, trusting that this prayer of faith would activate their miracle. I sat there in the parking lot for just a moment, struggling to grasp the magnitude of my mission. I had never done this before. What if I prayed and nothing happened? What if I stood by the bed and forgot how to speak the English language? What if he died while I was praying? I know that sounds incredibly bizarre but unfortunately it is true. There was still time to run, I thought. I even posed these inane questions to the Lord and He patiently listened. (In retrospect, I suspect that He may have smiled a little.) I honestly considered driving off in hopes that the resident chaplain would happen by the room and I would be relieved of this crushing responsibility. Realizing of course that flight was not a valid option, I slowly headed for the antiquated elevator, dutifully pressed the button and began a slow, uneasy climb. On the way up, I remember saying to the Lord, "Lord I'm out here on this limb. For this boy's sake, You had better be there."

The Lord loves limbs. That young man was wonderfully healed and is out and about today living life to its fullest. God truly performed a miracle for that young man (not because of me but in spite of me). That evening I had a decision to make: would I step out from the crowd and pray a true prayer of faith in the great healer or would I perform my obligatory ministerial duties and get out of Dodge? I climbed out on God's limb and He met us there in great power and great comfort for the patient, for the family, and for me. He is indeed a faithful God.

I am not foolish enough to compare my mustard seed faith with the mountain-moving faith of Elijah, but the principle is there. Such supernatural acts of faith do not happen by instantaneous combustion but by a conscious decision to stay in communication and communion with the Father through the Lord Jesus Christ by the power of the Holy Spirit. Day in, day out. First one limb and then another. Elijah had been well prepared for this day.

Let the work begin.

The second thing Elijah did in preparation for that grand finale was to repair the altar of the Lord that was broken down. Now remember this altar had likely *not* been destroyed by Jezebel but by carelessness and negligence on the part of the people of God. Under the watchful eye of the crowd, Elijah positioned first one stone and then another until all twelve stones were in place and the altar was complete.

In Elijah's case each of the twelve stones represented one of the tribes of Israel. By placing each stone one against another, one on top of another, one leaning strategically against the other the audience was given a visual reminder of their heritage, an awareness which had grown tragically faint and nearly fallen by the wayside. These witnesses were the direct descendants of the slaves delivered from Egypt through the mighty hand of God. Their ancestors, with all their flaws and imperfections, had seen evidence of God's provision and protection again and again and again, but a glaring oversight on their part had produced that weak, sinful generation present on Mount Carmel that day:

> *Deuteronomy 4:7-10, "⁷For what great nation is there that has God so near to it, as the Lord our God is to us, for whatever reason we may call upon Him? ⁸And what great nation is there that has such statutes and righteous judgments as are in all this law which I set before you this day? ⁹Only take heed to yourself, and diligently keep yourself, lest you forget the things your eyes have seen, and lest they depart from your heart all the days of your life. <u>And teach them to your children and your grandchildren,</u> ¹⁰ especially concerning the day you stood before the Lord your God in Horeb, when the Lord said to me, 'Gather the people to Me, and I will let them hear My words, that they may learn to fear Me all the days they live on the earth, <u>and that they may teach their children.</u>'"*

Well, what do you know? Somebody had forgotten to tell the kids.

> *Psalm 145:4, "⁴One generation shall praise Your works to another, and shall declare Your mighty acts."*

As a result of the negligence of generations gone by, those people who surrounded Elijah that day had become a nation of compromisers. They had not completely abandoned the worship of Jehovah, but they had begun to incorporate a deadly new component into their spiritual lives, that of human reasoning. Would it really do any harm to seek the favor of Baal, the reproductive god of crops and herds and flocks, for a little assistance with their yield?

It would be helpful if we could sit with one or two of these Israelites over a cup of coffee and ask them what in the world they were thinking. Seriously? Baal? We cannot do that, of course, but we have only to look at Scripture to see chunks of their story. Here are a few of the things that we can know from the Bible:

1. *They had become subject to the "everybody's doing it" syndrome.* As a united nation, previous generations had been virtually immersed in a society which exalted the one true God of Israel. The mixed multitude which had accompanied Israel out of Egypt in Moses' day brought with them some of their heathen beliefs, but they were a small minority. Now, however, their next door neighbors were often full-blown idolaters, those who were completely given over to Baal worship. At one time it was Israel's mark of distinction and notoriety that they worshipped only one God, but in this new many ways to God culture it became a mark of ignorance and intolerance.

Is this language ringing any bells for you in today's America?

2. *Reasoning* asks the question, is there really only one way to God? We tend to relate that question only to the days following Christ for He made that crystal clear:

John 14:6, "Jesus said to him, 'I am the way, the truth, and the life. No one comes to the Father, except through Me."

The "one way" principle had always been in effect, even prior to the Law, and those who unwaveringly subscribed to that one way had always been (and will always be) marked as fanatics, set aside, and hated by the world. One has only to peruse the book of Leviticus to appreciate the minute detail of acceptable worship under the Law; He left no margin for error in instruction. That exclusive worship requirement had been made abundantly known to the ancestors of the people who now surrounded Elijah, but from one generation to the next, the stringent demands and the resultant consequences had been diluted to the point that the present generation had no trepidation in violating that covenant. They apparently stood by that fallen altar with neither shame nor conviction.

3. *The sin nature of man turns a pleasing ear to any voice which issues forth a stamp of approval and a vestige of respectability to his sin, thereby relieving him of pangs of conscience.* Any ear attuned to the seductive voice of sin will become increasingly deaf to the conviction of the Holy Spirit. Many of the rites and rituals associated with the worship of Baal were inordinately lascivious, awakening the sensual desires for lewd practices and ceremonies absolutely forbidden to God's people, but if there were many gods or many ways to one God……..and the voice of conviction grew dimmer and dimmer and the voice of enticement of unbridled sexual indulgence grew louder and louder. Nearby stood the altar of the Lord, stark and desolate in its broken down state, a visible, tangible portrait of the hearts of God's people.

A nation is the sum of its citizens.

It might help us to view that scene from God's point of view. Since its birth as a nation there at the foot of Mount Sinai, the people of God had repeatedly fallen into destructive patterns of spiritual behavior, repeating the cycle over and over. The Lord would show Himself before them so grand and so powerful that the people would cry out, repent, and vow to follow after Jehovah, and only Jehovah, but their resolve was always short lived. Soon one of the greatest enemies of Israel and one of the greatest enemies of the church today would rear its ugly head: that of compromise. Since a nation is the sum of its citizens, the direction and spiritual health of Israel was dictated by the everyday choices of the men and women who populated its cities and countryside. One person at a time, one decision, one day, one household Baal god, one visit to the idolatrous rites and before long that man or that woman was hopelessly entrenched and enslaved.

The Lord was remarkably generous in speaking to them through the prophets and the great voices of chosen men, but ultimately He was compelled to take extraordinary measures to retrieve His people that He loved so much. Such was the circumstance which prompted Elijah's confrontational question, *"How long will you falter between two opinions?"* Their hateful idolatry and their lives of presumptuous sin had not gone unnoticed and Elijah was about to re-acquaint them with the God of their fathers. They would no longer need to draw upon the miraculous events of times gone by for they would soon have their own miracle to broadcast, and it would be their responsibility to teach the next generation.

History tells us that they did not.

The Lord, in His boundless, limitless beseeching, called out to man first in one way and then in another: as the husband of an unfaithful wife through the Prophet Hosea, as analogous backdrops through the heartrending prophecy of Jeremiah, and by shadowy visions in Ezekiel. A meditation upon the Word of God trumpets His all-consuming love and pursuit of man, even to the point of glimpses into the heart of our precious Lord.

Jeremiah 2:1-2, "¹Moreover the word of the Lord came to me, saying, ²'Go and cry in the hearing of Jerusalem,

saying, 'Thus says the Lord: I remember you, the kindness
of your youth, the love of your betrothal, when you went
after Me in the wilderness, in a land not sown.'"

The curse of sin pronounced at the time of the fall in the Garden of Eden ignited the perpetual rise and fall of the spiritual life of mankind. It would be woefully revealing to view that rise and fall in the way that we are able to view the output from an electrocardiograph, illustrating the peaks of blissful closeness interspersed by dark ravines of disobedience and separation. The stark cyclic path of man would be made painfully clear.

Did it have to be that way?

How vastly different might the story of Israel have been if each generation had simply been faithful to teach their kids, rather than allowing each generation to stumble in darkness at their own peril.

John 12:35, "³⁵Then Jesus said to them, 'A little while
longer the light is with you. Walk while you have the light,
lest darkness overtake you; he who walks in darkness does
not know where he is going.'"

That thick darkness, while not solely caused by our failure to pass truth on through generations, does impact our Christian walk. Without being taught the absolute truths of the Bible, we resemble Isaiah's description:

Isaiah 59:10, "¹⁰We grope for the wall like the blind, and
we grope as if we had no eyes: we stumble at noonday as in
the night; we are in desolate places as dead men."

We ought to learn from Israel, should we not? Should we not examine our own generation to determine just how faithful we have been in telling the kids the truth, the whole truth, and nothing but the truth which can be found only in the Word of God? Are we effectually equipping the next generation to face its challenges? Are we giving them the tools they will need to stand strong against the crushing societal weight which looms on the horizon? Or are we allowing our altar stones to deteriorate out of neglect and abuse as in the story of Elijah?

Our teaching leans heavily upon this visual picture of the twelve stones as they comprised Elijah's altar, with each stone examining a particular facet of life within the local church. There is a crippling weight of expectation placed upon our ministers to walk alike, look alike, think alike, sound alike, and even conform to a proper cadence of the voice from the pulpit. You know what I am talking about. Go to a restaurant on a Sunday afternoon and you can pick out the ministers from a mile away. Am I not right? We are producing Stepford servants. These are great men and women of God, called and equipped for the work but somebody forgot to tell the kids that they are each uniquely gifted and prepared to the particular field assigned to them by God Himself.

In Romans Chapter 12 Paul cautions us not to be conformed to this world. The expectation of the world system dictates that a person with a call upon their life should be spit-shined like the other, more successful guys in order to succeed. It teaches that you have to know the right language and demands that you be able to speak it fluently lest the other guys perceive you as less intellectual, not quite good enough for membership in the Stepford Country Club. Crushing pressure. Debilitating weight......in the beginning. But the more we conform, the less pressure we feel; the more we compromise who we really are in Christ, the less we feel like an outsider, and we are oh so glad to feel that pressure release and the next thing you know, we begin to embrace it.

Nonetheless, the moment we sacrifice our distinctiveness in Christ, we begin to experience a power drain. We know that because our Romans 12 scripture continues, *"...that you may prove what is that good and acceptable and perfect will of God*"[14] and then proceeds to methodically examine the individual gifts of the Father. Many members, one body in Christ.

While some may view these words as inflammatory, there is absolutely no such intent.

Instead, it is the goal of these teachings to encourage the blessed servants of God to waken to a new day, free from the ball and chain of religion and released to minister as the Holy Spirit leads them in their particular setting.

I am admittedly idealistic and an optimist at heart, but I am no fool. I know that these examinations are not a panacea for our American society; however, under the hand of the Holy Spirit, they can serve as creative launching pads for the servants of Christ. We live in extraordinarily perilous times, end times without a doubt, and the time is now for God's people to stand strong and firm, and – yes – to equip our kids to do likewise.

Let the altar restoration begin.

CHAPTER 3

STONE NUMBER 1: THE REVERENTIAL FEAR OF GOD

Proverbs 1:7, "⁷The fear of the Lord is the beginning of knowledge, but fools despise wisdom and instruction."

This one verse of Scripture may invoke more angst among believers than any other in the culture of today's American churches. Somewhere down through the ages the concept of reverential fear fell by the wayside and in its place sprung up a casual familiarity with God. To fear God, some would say, is to nullify the very provisions of grace. Are we not told in the New Testament that we can come boldly to the throne of *grace*? Are we not heirs of God, joint heirs with Christ? Should a man fear that One who became the captain of their salvation and who is not ashamed to openly call us His brethren?

Hebrews 2:11, "¹¹For both He who sanctifies and those who are being sanctified are all of one, for which reason He is not ashamed to call them brethren,"

The crux of the matter lies within the substance and intent of the word fear. It is that definition that we will address first because any teaching that we do on this matter rests squarely upon that understanding.

> Psalm 111:10, *"¹⁰ The fear of the Lord is the beginning of wisdom; a good understanding have all those who do His commandments. His praise endures forever."*

These words help us to frame in that line of thought. To fear God (or to give reverence to, to be in awe of, or to dread) opens the door to a level and range of spiritual wisdom which is otherwise inaccessible to man. "There are two main types of fear described by this word (fear): (a) the emotion and intellectual anticipation of harm, what one feels may go wrong for him; (b) a very positive feeling of awe or reverence for God which may be expressed in piety or formal worship."[15] True wisdom leads to reverence for God; reverence for God embarks man upon a spiritual journey of epic proportions, resulting in obedience which is the epitome of fruitfulness. The mere idea of drawing near to that divine throne absent grace would be a journey of terror, but Jesus Christ, our precious Savior, made a way.

Does that annul the call for fear in His presence? It absolutely does. Does that negate the need for reverence? To the contrary, it should result in an explosion of endless thanks and praise just as our Psalm 111 Scripture above says: *"His praise endures forever."*

Everyday life, a revealing portrait

What happens to a society which refuses to fear God? You need look no further than your own city, state, and nation. Fear strikes at the heart of America's citizens, ranging from mild anxiety or negative anticipation to phobias so strong as to incapacitate its victims. Extreme phobias of such a magnitude as to cripple lives affect some 11.5 million people in America.[16] In recent years a television show appeared on the scene which affectionately explored the life of a man controlled by his irrational fears and did so with great humor, only occasionally giving the viewer a glimpse into the true torture these precious men and women endure.

The most powerful instance of truly phobic behavior I have ever witnessed took place at a high school graduation many years ago. The ceremony convened in a very crowded gymnasium/auditorium on a hot, humid day. Every attendee grabbed a copy of the program to use as a feeble fan, moving some of that heavy air around. Speeches were delivered; awards were given and then began the interminable calling of individual student names. Anyone who has ever attended one of these graduation ceremonies knows exactly what I am talking about. Graduate after graduate climbed up two four-inch steps, walked slowly across the beautifully decorated platform, received his or her congratulatory handshake and photo op, stepped back down two four-inch steps assisted by an underclassman and then the next name was called. Did I mention the class was really, really big? Somewhere about halfway through the roster, the name of a particular young man was called and he proceeded up the steps. He was a handsome young man, tall and strong with a Marlboro man kind of appearance. He crossed the platform, received his diploma, smiled for his picture, and walked to the two small descending steps. Then he froze. It took a few minutes for anyone to realize what was happening, but a fear of heights had come upon him (whether temporary or chronic is unknown) and those two little steps must have looked like a ledge on the top of the Sears Tower to him. Try as he might, he just could not bring himself to step down. As school officials began to grasp the magnitude of his problem they began to try to talk him down so to speak, but to no avail. The boy was horribly embarrassed, the officials were bumfuzzled, and the crowd was on the edge of their collective seats trying to help the boy as an observer might work hard to assist a wrestler on the mat. They tried reasoning, but you do not reason with a phobia. Several minutes went by before one wise teacher stepped forward and instructed the young man to move back from the edge and sit down on the platform and then he (the teacher) crawled on all fours to sit by his side, helping him to scoot on his posterior to the edge where he could easily plant his feet on the floor.

An extreme instance? Perhaps, but it was a visual demonstration in the physical of a powerful, unaddressed mental and emotional stronghold. With one shift in his thinking that young man could easily have walked off that platform just like all the rest of the students. As a worst-case scenario he might have landed awkwardly on an ankle and sustained a minor sprain but arriving at that conclusion would have required logical reasoning, an exercise diametrically opposed to the grip of fear, anxieties, and phobias. Thank God for clergy, physicians, and counselors who extend helping hands of compassion and healing to those men and women who are held in such bondage.

The gamut of fear

We begin with this example of extreme fear in order to set the boundaries for our study. Fear, in and of itself, is a God-given response necessary for the preservation of mankind. Pause for a moment to consider your own life….absent fear. "We are so used to portrayals of neurotics crippled by a million anxieties that we seldom stop to think what would happen if we had none at all."[17]

Fear's hold on mankind runs the gamut with the extreme stranglehold of phobias on one end of the spectrum to the everyday fears on the other. Some of those fears are life-preserving warnings whose observance protects us and keeps us alive and then there are those which we experience without giving them so much as a by-the-by. For instance: I fear that the snowstorm predicted for tonight may keep me from my appointed schedule tomorrow morning; you might fear that gas prices will rise right before your next road trip or that the line at Starbucks will cause you to be late for work; I fear that some of you from other regions of the country will not be familiar with bumfuzzling.

Somewhere in the middle of that continuum – between crippling phobias and everyday fears – we experience anxieties. You may know anxiety by other names such as fretting, stewing, troubled, or fussing. A rose by any other name.

Every family in America has been touched by fears and anxieties on some level and as a society we apparently find some perverse gratification in observing such burdened behavior. Thus, the reality show epidemic currently raging. Our immersion in fear and anxiety stretches way beyond individuals and family units, however, for we have become a nation of fearful, apprehensive people. Twenty-four hour news stations (whose very existence depends upon perpetual breaking news) stoke the fires of terror and sound the alarm anew every thirty minutes just in case you missed it last time; politicians of every conviction rely upon invoking fear among common citizens; stories of unthinkable horror (both real and fictional) rush before our faces with remarkable speed and frequency from the television screen and the internet. The world responds to such triggers as one would expect: fearfully, and that is exactly what we should expect for they walk through life, either willfully or ignorantly, without a reverent fear of God. Remember, without a reverential fear of God who holds the key to all spiritual wisdom, man staggers to and fro like a man without sight or hearing, dependent upon his own flawed understanding. And that really *is* scary stuff.

I must resist the tendency to focus on the world, however, because as you recall, we are not interested in assessing the world right now. They are just doing what the world does, remember? What you and I do need to do is to invite the Holy Spirit to examine us without reservation. Your everyday life broadcasts your level of reverence toward God, either to His glory or to His disdain. What does your life say?

What I say is thank God for grace! With His help, we can become a body of people standing strong in the power of His might and declare the words of Abraham, Isaac, Jacob, Moses, and Samuel as they each cried out in their own generation, "Here am I." Oh that He would raise up men and women who are willing to pay the price to follow the example of Isaiah when he cried out, "Here am I, Lord. Send me." It may be that our generation will be the one to restore the altar stones in preparation for the manifest power of God, just like Elijah did.

Do not lose sight of our ultimate goal which is to answer the provocative, two-pronged question: Is the church in America largely ineffective because of the depraved state of our society? Or is our society in that corrupt state because the church is largely ineffective? As we carefully position this first altar stone perhaps we can begin to shed some light on the answer.

One stone strategically placed

This first altar stone (that of the reverential fear of God) provides the placement for each of the other stones since that is the beginning of wisdom. In other words, if we neglect to take the time for a proper grasp and understanding of the stone of reverential fear the remaining eleven stones will be precariously poised, causing the believer to become unstable. Elijah's mother and father must have been among those who did comprehend that reverence because they named their son "Jehovah is my God."

It is crucial to point out that the cross became the ultimate and final altar as the Lamb of God laid down His life thereupon. There will be no second option for salvation; no further bloodshed. As you will recall, the use of these altar stones for illustration is based upon the preparation by Elijah, the man of God, in anticipation of the undeniable move of God in the presence of all the people. Likewise (if we are willing to be obedient) the Lord will grant our fervent petitions that we too might witness a great move of God, and (as on Mount Carmel) He will do so in clear view of all the people.

> *Romans 2:4, "⁴ Or do you despise the riches of His goodness, forbearance, and longsuffering, not knowing that the goodness* (the goodness, kindness, graciousness) *of God leads you to repentance?"*

Abraham's first altar

Some of the Old Testament altars were built, not as sacrificial altars, but as altars of memorial to the greatness of God or as a tribute and perpetual monument to one specific divine act. The first altar of Abraham, for instance, seems to have been built as such a tribute:

> Genesis 12:7, "⁷Then the Lord appeared to Abram and said, 'To your descendants I will give this land.' And there he built an altar to the Lord, who had appeared to him."

This altar appears to have been one of memorial in response to the divine communication of the promise: *"To your descendants I will give this land."* It is an unfortunate truth that the word of the Lord to one man is rarely fully appreciated by another man. You may remember a time in your life when the Lord spoke to you clearly and tenderly a word that altered your circumstance, redirected your steps, or even changed your life. That word was like a precious jewel, treasured and cherished and you could hardly contain your excitement until you could share that word with someone close to you. As you poured out your heart to that friend or even to your pastor, they likely responded with a smile and an obligatory, "How nice." Their lack of appreciation probably took some of the wind out of your sails, but it should not because that was *your* word or *your* promise, not theirs. When God told Abram that he would give that land to his descendants it meant something to Abram that you and I simply cannot grasp. His altar was built to give tribute and honor to Jehovah God who not only had made a promise but was well able to deliver on that promise. By building that altar Abram accomplished two objectives:

1. First and foremost to give glory to God for that which was yet to come.

2. Second, to leave on that earthly landscape a visible, tangible witness of the unassailable word of God to generations to come, the very descendants to whom God would give this land. That was but one marker of the legacy that Abram, soon to become Abraham, would leave for his descendants, both natural and spiritual.

What can Abraham's commemorative altar of stone teach us in America today? How can that lesson help us to restore the altar stone of reverential fear? Abraham felt compelled to construct that place of remembrance for future generations. Compelled? By whom? By what motivation? What was it which drove him? We cannot know with certainty Abraham's mind in that matter, but we are able, inside the teachings of Scripture, to ascertain certain pieces of that puzzle. For instance, Abraham worshiped Jehovah God prior to the great promises. He did not worship God to cash in on the promises of God but received great promises because he was a worshiper. How and why did he become a worshiper of the One True God? We do not know that answer definitively. However, we do know that his divine command and his promise were given some five generations after the Tower of Babel and hundreds of years following the days of the great flood. There is absolutely no doubt that the no nonsense reputation of this Jehovah God was common knowledge among the nations. His unsurpassed deeds must have been a topic of conversation around campfires, in the fields, in the market place, and around kitchen tables far and wide. By word of mouth, His deeds had passed from generation to generation, leaving the hearer to make his or her own choice. Some, like Abraham, heard, believed, and worshiped, while others, also having heard, chose to reject reverential fear and turned instead to worship dumb idols. So will it be in our own society. The harvest is His:

> *Luke 10:2, "² Then He said to them, 'The harvest truly is great, but the laborers are few; therefore pray the Lord of the harvest to send out laborers into His harvest."*

Some will hear and accept; others will not. Our part is to live our lives in such a way as to cause others to acknowledge an all-powerful, almighty, fearsome, eternal God who has extended Himself toward mankind with grace, beneficence, compassion, and unconditional love through the blood of the Lamb of God who died on that final altar of the cross.

We are beneficiaries of Abraham's memorial altar as surely as his natural descendants. With him as one of our supreme examples of obedience to God, then how much more should we do likewise, not by the erection of a physical altar for that day is gloriously past and settled, but by worshiping, living, succeeding, prospering, and speaking the language of reverential worship.

> *Hebrews 2:1, "¹ Therefore we must give the more earnest heed to the things we have heard, lest we drift away."*

The measure of the absence or presence of reverential fear can be a bit thorny for by what standard do we gauge, what do we use as a benchmark? Sometimes a question is most clearly countered with another question and that is the approach that we will take here.

The role of reverential fear in church attendance

1. Would a believer in an all-seeing, all-knowing, all-powerful God fall prey to a lackadaisical approach to church attendance? While not a condition of salvation, it most certainly is a statement of the expectation of the believer for the "*fear of the Lord is the beginning of wisdom*" and, and as we have already established, it opens the door to wisdom and understanding not accessible from any other source. A person who confesses Christ and is openly known to the world as a believer faces troubles and trials in this lifetime the same as the lost. The key difference is that we have a refuge and we have an advocate. That puts us on

totally different planes. However, if the world sees us struggling just as they do in the midst of trials, then what is the advantage of being a Christian? If our God is not able to sustain us, why should they desire Him? Picture if you will a believer who wakes up on a Sunday morning thankful for the grace that allows him to stay in bed. Now imagine that same believer saved by grace but this time, add just a tablespoon of reverential fear and that is the man who will be walking through the church doors ready to take his place with fellow believers, well-rounded in his responsive service to the Lord.

The role of reverential fear in staying put

2. Should a Christian be unwilling or spiritually unable to commit to a local body? There is an epidemic of church-hopping in America today causing instability, frustrating pastors, and handicapping the work of the church. Spiritual gifts are dormant, unable to be thoroughly activated for lack of covering.

    Ephesians 4:11-12, "[11]And He Himself gave some to be apostles, some prophets, some evangelists, and some pastors and teachers, [12]for the equipping of the saints for the work of ministry, for the edifying of the body of Christ."

    An hourglass gives us an accurate depiction of the life of the body of Christ. Having received spiritual gifts from the Father as listed in Romans Chapter 12 (the top of the glass), the believer is directed to submit to the leadership of the apostles, prophets, evangelists, pastors, and teachers called by God for the work of ministry, for the edifying of the body of Christ (the constricted middle of the glass). Having prayerfully submitted to a local pastor, then the gifts of the Spirit listed in 1st Corinthians

Chapter 12, can be released and the believer can rightly walk and flourish.

I clearly recall one memorable Sunday morning a very long time ago which never fails to make me smile. A very dear couple, good friends of ours, was seated directly in front of us during the morning service. They were caring for a very active two year old, the son of another family, and the woman had come prepared with a little goodie bag filled with items that would help occupy the child's attention during the services. As the pastor preached the message, I noticed that the little boy had removed all the goodies from the tote and proceeded to put the bag upside down over his head. Just in the nick of time, the woman realized what he was doing and she removed the bag, quietly shook her head, and returned her attention to the message. The child promptly picked up the bag and repeated his transgression; she quickly repeated the scolding. On about the fourth try, the child succeeded in pulling the tote so far down that the opening rested directly upon his shoulders with his entire head lodged inside. The woman casually glanced to her left and suddenly realized that the boy's head was completely stuck inside the container as he thrashed frantically in an attempt to loose himself. She really did try to stay calm and nonchalant so as not to disturb the whole congregation but it is hard to hide a kid with a sack stuck on his head, and the harder she pulled on that bag the more chaotic it became. In desperation, she picked up the child and rushed him out of the sanctuary, bag still lodged on the head. A palpable wave of laughter rolled over that sizable congregation as she carried that baby through the sanctuary and out the door. The child with the sack on his head was completely clueless, but that sermon mostly fell on deaf ears that morning.

Failing to recognize your gift of the Father, neglecting to submit that gift to the leadership of a local church, or attempting to move in the gifts of the Spirit without accountability will result in just such a manner, muddled and frenzied, much like the little boy with the sack on his head, and yet that is what we in America do. Gone is the neighborhood church where families planted roots, raised their children, and saw generation after generation grow up behind them. Gone are the times when families remained under the compassionate hand of the neighborhood pastor whose heart was to equip the saints "*for the work of ministry, for the edifying of the body of Christ.*"

I once heard it said that you should always watch both hands of a con man and not just the hand that he is working with openly (such as the pea under the shell). That working hand is just to distract your eye from what he is really up to with the other hand. Satan has successfully whispered into the ear of many a Christian in America words such as these:

a. You do not really *need* to commit to a local body. They just want your money.

b. You do not have to submit yourself to any man's authority. You are an American, you are a free spirit, and you do not need anyone to tell you what you can or cannot do or should or should not do.

c. God is everywhere. You can worship under the oak tree in the backyard. Why should you sit down with hypocrites, because we all know that the church is full of those?

d. You know that if you do become a part of the local church you will only get hurt again, just like before.

Always watch the other hand. While he occupies your mind with such trivial nonsense as this, his other hand is stealing your joy, your witness, the loving support of brothers and sisters in the Lord, the great comfort of knowing that there are those who are watching for your soul, and (above all) he is damaging your communion with God. A reverential fear of God immediately nullifies every iota of validity to the above whispers. Point by point it replies:

a. We are the body of Christ, He being the Head of the body. A reverential fear of God reminds us that the church is His plan and not the plan of any man. Therefore, to eschew commitment to a local body is to disparage His plan.

b. Finding that local church where God's plan for your life can be activated is not a decision to be taken lightly. Pursue Him, chase after His counsel, ask for His wisdom and then once He has given you direction, commit, stay put, put down roots, work through any bumps in the road, and resolve to remain and be fruitful. That same all powerful God who manifested His might on Mount Carmel is at work in your life. Fear the One whose fire consumed the sacrifice, the wood, the stones, and the dust around Elijah's altar, and then by grace, call out "Abba" or "Daddy" to that same God and watch Him race to your rescue. Balance, balance, balance.

c. Worshiping under an oak tree can be a profound experience for truly His creation speaks all around us, and so let us not denigrate the practice of worshiping God wherever we are. Neither can we say that a building is necessary for the worship of God; we all know that it is not. Robert Louis Stevenson once described for us the citizens of an infamous leper colony where the repellent malady and its ensuing mutilation co-existed daily alongside great inward beauty and resilience. The two contrasting extremes were intimately knit. Similarly, the church is made up of imperfect people, once horribly disfigured by sin, who have now been made the righteousness of Christ, *"knit together in love".*[18]

2nd Corinthians 5:21, "21 For He made Him who knew no sin to be sin for us, that we might become the righteousness of God in Him."

We are one body, each with strengths and with weaknesses, but we are stronger together. Aside from man's relationship with God, there are certain elements of life which are central to the happiness and total health of man. Secular psychology delineates these as the ability to motivate ourselves, the ability to persist against frustration, the ability to delay gratification, the ability to regulate moods, the presence of hope, the ability to empathize with others, and the ability to control impulses.

These elements, crucial to the health and well-being of man are birthed and developed by abiding in the safe shelter of the body of Christ, covered by the Head, under compassionate earthly leadership. There iron sharpens iron and there these various traits can be finely honed. To what end?

Ephesians 4:15-16, "15 but, speaking the truth in love, may grow up in all things into Him who is the head – Christ – 16 from whom the whole body, joined and knit together by what every joint supplies, according to the effective working by which every part does it share, causes growth of the body for the edifying of itself in love."

A reverential fear of God, an awestruck heart if you will, draws us to that place of growth and maturity. A comprehension of the unconditional love of God and His mercy and grace in concert with the love of our brothers and sisters (imperfect though it might be) keeps us there.

d. I cannot count the times down through the years of ministry when I have heard the sincere cry, "I have been hurt by hypocrites over and over, and I will not let it happen again. I will just stay home and watch TV preachers and that way I won't get hurt again." While most of us can identify with that sentiment because of our own past wounds, it is seriously flawed thinking for you most certainly *will* experience hurt there - of a different variety perhaps - but hurt nonetheless. Let me give you an example of a very superficial wound. There was a time in my life when we were searching for a home church for the short term. The Lord had already spoken that we would be leaving the area but there was a delay of nearly a year. In the meantime we decided to take refuge in a sizable local church with a reputation for being a dynamic welcoming congregation. Arriving just as Sunday School was preparing to dismiss we sidled down the outside aisle inconspicuously taking a seat in the auditorium which probably accommodated two to three thousand. We hardly had time to warm up the seats before a young mother with two small children and a very large bad attitude approached. "That is my pew. My family sits here. You will need to move."

Whereupon she turned on her heel and marched off in a huff. In my younger days I would probably have called her on it but old age does have its benefits and on this day we quietly removed ourselves to another vacant area and worshiped the Lord. Hurts come. Hypocrites exist. "If the primary aim of a captain were to preserve his ship, he would keep it in port forever." (Thomas Aquinas) The goal is *not* to stay pain-free forever, but to mature in the Lord and to learn to handle wrongs in a way that builds and does not tear down. A balance of reverential fear and His wonderful mercy and grace will keep us in times of hurt and supply the wisdom we need to perpetuate a healthy local body. Come out from under your oak tree of protection and take your rightful place in the body.

The role of reverential fear in training our children

3. Our final question in the search to gauge the absence or presence of reverential fear in our local churches today is this: How is it possible that a born-again believer could feel no compulsion to train up his or her children in the ways of the Lord? How is it possible that we relegate our children's spiritual upbringing to a world system in fierce opposition to the ways of God? It cannot be laid at the foot of grace for grace leaves us with an overwhelming desire to prostrate ourselves before Him out of sheer gratitude. It is the absence of reverential fear which numbs our hearts and minds of His greatness and wonder, leaving the enemy of God to seduce us into one of several excuses such as: the child will learn on his own when he is older; the pastor can teach him; I don't know how and I don't have time to figure it out. The fact that such excuses actually lull us into a sense of ease speaks volumes about our level of reverential fear. I leave

you to mull this over for a while because we will study it at some length in another section, but it seems that the answer is self-apparent for we see it all around us.

We have now examined three simple areas common to all believers and attempted to establish these as indicators of the level of respect and reverence exercised in our lives. The possibilities for other areas of evidences and proof are endless, but these three (church attendance, local church commitment, and faithfulness in teaching children) are quickly relatable to any Christian in America. Another indicator, just as universal as the previous three but much broader in scope can be found, of all places, in our music.

Music: The universal language

Music is an inborn part of the fabric of man as beings created by God. Our tastes and preferences may vary, but music has the ability to move us all, and it was a vital part of the life of the nation of Israel. Small wonder, then, that music was such a central component of their everyday life and the holy feasts of the nation.

Israel's spiritual life followed a cyclic pattern following the division of the nation into the northern and southern kingdoms. Serve God, serve idols; serve God, and then become as the adulterous wife. Two modern day adventurers wrote in their journal narrative as they traversed the Nile that it was not one particular misstep which caused them so much angst, but a series of little slips. Such was the case with Israel. Under godly leadership they were at peace and prospered and their worship was directed to the one true God, but little slip by little slip the people chose to look and act like neighboring idolatrous nations and repeatedly fell into the practice of idolatry. Their sin always resulted in a national (never pleasant) call to repentance followed by a restoration of proper worship and service, again and again and time after time. One of the signposts along their personal roundabout can be seen in their music, memorials to both the glory of their God and to their darkened hope. For instance, when King David proclaimed Solomon as the one who would rule in his stead the people rejoiced with a celebration that rocked the world:

> *1ˢᵗ Kings 1:39-40, "³⁹ Then Zadok the priest took a horn of oil from the tabernacle and anointed Solomon. And they blew the horn, and all the people said, 'Long live King Solomon!' ⁴⁰ And all the people went up after him; and the people played the flutes and rejoiced with great joy, so that the earth seemed to split with their sound."*

At that point in history, the people (as a nation) were following after God, walking in reverential awe and wonder at His greatness and His might. This celebration not only honored King David and Solomon but it acknowledged that God Himself had provided an heir to the throne and *"the earth seemed to split with their sound."*

Years later King Solomon set about to fulfill the charge as he began construction on the Temple:

> *2ⁿᵈ Chronicles 6:7-9, "⁷ Now it was in the heart of my father David to build a temple for the name of the Lord God of Israel. ⁸ But the Lord said to my father David, 'Whereas it was in your heart to build a temple for My name, you did well in that it was in your heart.*
> *⁹ Nevertheless you shall not build the temple, but your son who will come from your body, he shall build the temple for My name.'"*

Our focus is not the construction of the temple, but the explosive worship which accompanied its dedication as the fire fell from heaven, consuming the burnt offering and the sacrifices. The glory of the Lord so filled the house that the people (of their own volition) worshiped the Lord:

2ⁿᵈ Chronicles 7:6, "⁶ And the priests attended to their services; the Levites also with instruments of the music of the Lord, which King David had made to praise the Lord, saying, 'For His mercy endures forever,' whenever David offered praise by their ministry. The priests sounded trumpets opposite them, while all Israel stood."

Quite a scene. Who would have believed that their descendants would later sing a much different song as they took another lap on the roundabout:

Psalm 137:1-4, "¹By the rivers of Babylon, There we sat down, yea, we wept when we remembered Zion. ²We hung our harps upon the willows in the midst of it. ³For there those who carried us away captive asked of us a song, and those who plundered us requested mirth, Saying, 'Sing us one of the songs of Zion!' ⁴How shall we sing the Lord's song in a foreign land?"

The Jews were widely known as the only people who worshiped one God; all the other nations had many, one for every occasion. The nation was recognized far and wide for her songs of praise to Jehovah God, and it was that very renown that brought about these taunts. "Sing us a song," their captors would decry. "Tell us about this great and mighty God of yours. Tell us about how He brought your ancestors out of Egypt with a mighty hand." Their songs of worship and celebration consistently embraced certain aspects:

1. They extolled the Lord, lifting His name to the heavens in order that other peoples and other nations might see and hear and believe. (Psalm 145:1)

2. They exalted God, praising His name, His person, His character, and His boundless excellence above all gods of the imaginations

of man. This exaltation drove away fears and reminded man of His mercy and His sovereignty (Psalm 34, Psalm 118, Isaiah 25).

3. They glorified Him, proclaiming to the world the splendor of Jehovah God, lifting His name far beyond the plane of any other power. Their worship, by word and by song, painted a stunning portrait of the God of Israel, a beautiful portrayal of their adoration with a centerpiece of reverential fear.

So went the music of Israel, but what does our own music say about us? And how does that relate to the fear of the Lord?

When Martin Luther posted his theses in 1517 he did not comprehend, nor could he have ever imagined what would follow. The ensuing turmoil and turbulence among church leaders of the day, painful as they were, culminated in our own liberty to worship:

> *Ephesians 2:8-9, "⁸For by grace you have been saved through faith, and that not of yourselves; it is the gift of God, ⁹ not of works, lest anyone should boast."*

That newly realized liberty to worship, purchased at such an agonizing cost, was not limited to the spoken word as it was now received by the masses, but it extended into the worship as well. Music has always been the language of loving hearts reaching out to a fervently receptive divine God. The music which accompanied the corporate worship of that and ensuing centuries reflected the Creator/creature dynamic at work as we see in this early hymn first published in 1561, only forty-four years following Luther's world-changing act:

> All people that on earth do dwell,
> Sing to the Lord with cheerful voice;
> Him serve with fear, His praise forth tell,
> Come ye before Him and rejoice.[19]

Notwithstanding the awkward old English, can you see the revered distance of the worshiper? The passionate desire is not lessened by that veneration but is actually enhanced and magnified. Watch the grandeur of our next hymn, which came to be in the early 1700's:

> Lo! He comes, with clouds descending,
> Once for favored sinners slain;
> Thousand, thousand saints attending
> Swell the triumph of His train;
> Hallelujah! Hallelujah! Hallelujah!
> God appears on earth to reign,
> God appears on earth to reign.[20]

By this time man had begun to grasp the magnitude of the doctrine of justification by faith, moving further and further from the early roots in Catholicism. The music began to reflect man's comprehension of the unfathomable love of God toward man and the unbroken and unhindered accessibility of communication and communion. That joyful understanding began to surface in song:

> Depth of mercy! Can there be
> Mercy still reserved for me?
> Can my God His wrath forbear,
> Me, the chief of sinners, spare?[21]

And of course no such survey can be made without including this beloved standard:

> Amazing grace! How sweet the sound
> That saved a wretch like me!
> I once was lost but now am found,
> Was blind but now I see.[22]

The author of "Amazing Grace" once responded to inquiries about his advanced age in this manner: "My memory is nearly gone, but I remember two things: that I am a great sinner, and that Christ is a great Savior." Written in 1725, this song has blessed and continues to bless generations of Christians by giving voice both to a groaning awareness of man's depravity and absolute confidence in the amazing grace of God in His redemption of mankind.

By the 1800's we can see a further progression and a level of comfort in His presence heretofore not seen in public assemblies and yet still there was a distance, a level of reverence and enthrallment that reached for the stars:

> Crown him with many crowns,
> The Lamb upon His throne;
> Hark! How the heavenly anthem drowns
> All music but its own.
> Awake, my soul, and sing
> Of Him who died for thee,
> And hail Him as thy matchless King
> Through all eternity.[23]

Compare that 1800's consciousness of His majesty with another of that same period and you will see the compatibility of reverential fear and amazing grace melding together into a wonderful harmony:

> Face to face with Christ my Savior, face to face – what will it be?
> When with rapture I behold Him, Jesus Christ who died for me!
> Face to face I shall behold Him, far beyond the starry sky;
> Face to face, in all His glory, I shall see Him by and by![24]

Did you notice a new aspect of the grace relationship reflected in that stanza? At some point in our history writers of hymns began to give more and more voice to the assurance that His grace was sufficient to see us through to an eternity with Him, i.e., *I shall see him by and by.* The petition had rightly changed from one of distant pleading to one of restful praise and thanksgiving.

Although hymns of every age gave witness to the ever present Holy Spirit, it was not until much later that the music of the church reflected the sweet personal relationship available to every Christian. Consider the longing for closeness and familiarity expressed in the following song which was written in the late 1700's:

> Holy Ghost, with light divine
> Shine upon this heart of mine;
> Chase the shades of night away,
> Turn my darkness into day
>
> Holy Spirit, all divine,
> Dwell within this heart of mine;
> Cast down ev'ry idol throne,
> Reign supreme and reign alone.[25]

Now contrast those lyrics with the ease with which we revel in the closeness and assurance of the presence of the Holy Spirit today. An enormous difference. That is not to say that those saints of centuries past were somehow more or less spiritual than we are today for that is sheer nonsense; witness the names and faces of the great men and women of God of times gone by and how often we draw from their lives and words as we sing, write, and preach. What we can learn is the way in which the evolution of public worship has served as a barometer of the reverential fear of the believer, and a mirror reflecting the everyday life of the people during that time. Even in the recent history of the United States we can see this principle at work. A renowned lyricist by the name of George Bennard gave voice to a profound truth by recognizing that the inspiration for his music was planted in his heart in response to needs in his own life in much the same way that certain music touches our heart because of our own life experiences. Mr. Bennard's most famous work, *"The Old Rugged Cross,"* continues to be one of America's favorite hymns to this day. Even as music called to its composer in the time of his or her own need, so does music respond to the culture in which it is embedded.

Musical composition in the church took yet other extraordinary turns in more recent times. Remember Bennard's thought? The same individual principle was at work on a societal level. The need of the society drove the music and, conversely, music had the power to elevate the society. With World War I in its recent national memory, songs such as this one began to ring through the sanctuaries of America:

> Great is Thy faithfulness!
> Great is Thy faithfulness!
> Morning by morning new mercies I see;
> All I have needed Thy hand hath provided--
> Great is Thy faithfulness, Lord, unto me![26]

There was a new mindfulness of an eternal, spiritual destination, a consciousness of heaven and the eternal glory which awaits the true believer:

> *1st Peter 5:10, "10But the God of all grace, who hath called us unto his eternal glory by Christ Jesus, after that ye have suffered a while, make you perfect, stablish, strengthen, settle you."*

Americans in the early to mid-1900s were searching, in dogged pursuit of some fountain of optimism in the midst of chaos and turmoil. Catastrophic loss in the natural realm had spawned a deep sense of emptiness, a profound void which could not be satisfied by re-acquiring wealth or possessions or any other earthbound consolation. Once again the Holy Spirit moved ever so sweetly upon the hearts and minds of the lyricists and musicians of the day and they rose to the occasion declaring by their works that their tongues were the pens of ready writers.[27] What followed were songs of declaration of endless hope, health, happiness, joy, peace, and timeless comfort in His presence. The joyful rain of those eternal reminders was so powerful as to be almost tangible when our congregations sang them out. Stories were handed down from generation to generation of families who parked their cars just outside the open windows of these churches so that they could hear these sweet songs of promise. They were not quite ready to go inside, but they could not resist His gentle beckoning to hear of an end to the chaos of this world and the promise of the eternal home to come.

Particular longings flowed from the hearts of entire populations of oppressed African-Americans during that same period. From the urban street corners to the narrow wood-sided churches of the south, congregations lifted up voices of hope. The ever-present, ever searching Holy Spirit spoke through the great writers of the day, sending forth high praise extolling the approaching blissful day in the presence of a perfectly just God. It may indeed have been the broad audience of these spirituals which began to bring a first-person awareness of that brutal oppression into the highly segregated white churches.

Time marched on and World War II erupted. The heart and soul of the nation cried out through the time of loss and sacrifice, searching the horizon for better days through Christ Jesus. Unlike previous recent decades which rang of eternal destiny, the music of that period focused more heavily upon the sustaining presence of God from day to day upon this earth. Families bidding farewell to foreign-soil bound soldiers relied upon His power and His omnipresence to guard over their loved ones, and so the music responded to the need. Things may go bad again. War lurks forever upon the horizon. Great depressions may come and go. Oppressions seem to always be with us in some form or another, but that generation gathered together across the land roaring out in song Sunday after Sunday that Jesus is alive and well and very much involved in the affairs of man.

Along came the 1950's, the decade so applauded by many of our young people. The Korean Conflict was raging in the early part of that decade, but the worship music of that time seems to reflect more concern about a new threat: materialism, an early-stage plague which would eventually devour our culture. There were very few new songs written during that period which trumpeted the coming eternal kingdom and the confessional songs of His daily provision were mostly left over from previous years. In their place we sang songs of confirmation in the supremacy of worship over the possession of goods. Stuff cannot satisfy; stuff cannot save, but godliness with contentment, now that is true gain.[28]

The decade of the 60's is one that we mostly want to tuck away in the hallway closet in unmarked boxes. During those years eclipsed by the Vietnam debacle, we said goodbye to brothers and sisters, mothers and fathers, friends, and even fellow Americans to whom we felt a kinship simply by common birth. They left without fanfare and if they returned at all, they came back wounded and distressed to an inhospitable nation. Every family in our nation was touched by that conflict in very personal ways. We were left with bloody schisms in families, among friends, and even within the walls of the churches across our nation. The streets were full of violence and our government was (depending upon your stance) either unwilling or unable to put an end to the brutal beast which stalked our young men and women. Somebody had to pay a price. Somebody had to shoulder the responsibility. Our nation was reeling. Indeed there were some songs of the Lord written during this period but there was a noticeable lull, as though the wind had been sucked out of our sails. And so it had.

Generational genre vs. worship wonder

This journey through the hymns of the ages in no way endorses or disparages any particular style or genre of music. It is merely intended as a tool to assist us in our examination of music as an expression of its host society. When Christians of any society have a pure, balanced view of the God they worship, then reverential fear will drive a steadying stake in that worship allowing it to reach heights unachievable in its absence for our worship must not depend upon an external trigger such as music; it must be an expression of heartfelt worship which inevitably manifests itself in music.

Let's consider the music of today and see if we can trace its outlook and perspective. In order to keep the path of our study consistent, however, we need to start with an examination of the society out of which it is birthed and from which it rings. The national median age of America's population is fixed at 36.8 years.[29] From my personal vantage point, just about everybody seems young, but 36.8 really *is* young. This present generation of Americans faces a whole army of noxious Goliaths and there seems to be a sharp awareness on the part of our young people that the present "just-get-by" dragon of the church has to be slain. Their music reaches forward with immediacy, lyrically proclaiming the need for action, courage, fearlessness, change, and militancy, and small wonder. Unspeakable brutality blares its voice from the evening news. Horrifying deeds that previous generations would never have imagined have become the norm. Hopelessness forms a bleak horizon for the next generation. These young people are bombarded with catastrophic prognostications on all sides. Civility has nearly disappeared from our midst. Politics has become nothing short of barbaric. Fast-paced living is touted as the panacea to all your problems. Run faster. Run harder. Do more. Go more. The fulfillment and success of your life, we say, is only as good as the level of your activity.

One contemporary artist described today's Christian music as almost disposable, and why not? Our spiritual legacy to these brave and wonderful young Christians is a national disgrace and embarrassment. We have handed them a nation where the very existence of God is disputed and where Christianity is viewed as a definable political force rather than the loving and compassionate, visible body of Christ. For them, religion is portrayed as an empty, lifeless, bothersome option and not a matter of eternal destination. Mystical ideals have extended idolatrous hands to show the way to peace and contentment and even the church has responded to the pressure of inclusion.

It is in this atmosphere of chaos and confusion that today's Christian composers find themselves – perhaps unwittingly - living out Bennard's words, music which answers to the need of the culture in which it is birthed.

The bleeding wounds of this generation cry out for the touch of a loving Father, one which will bring relief from the emptiness, the uncertainty, and the loneliness that every sunrise brings. The love of Christians in this generation for the one true God is unbelievably passionate and focused, perhaps in response to the very pressures spoken of earlier. This generation is prepared to do battle if necessary. The music reflects a need to fight back, and not only to fight but to be victorious, fueling this almost frenetic worship. The one hope this generation has of regaining some sort of undefined equilibrium is to win this fight.

The 1970's and 80's brought more confrontational music, songs which spoke loudly of the spiritual battle around us and our role in fighting that fight. The music gave a face to the battle at hand but it also began to accentuate the prominence of the contribution of the human element while losing sight of the One whose very name instills fear in His enemies. As generations once built upon the glorious comprehension of grace and justification by faith, we raced to give our children an intimate relationship with a one-dimensional God.

As a result of all of these factors – and ever so much more – today's music focuses heavily upon the individual and his or her role in moving the hand of God, making it perfectly clear that they intend to do what previous generations either could not or would not do.

Nothing wrong with that; David did it. He did not hesitate to call upon the mighty hand of God, but there was an oft-repeated structure to David's compositions. First of all, He was honest with God, uninhibited in speaking words that flow as from the heart of a child. David was not handicapped out of fear that someone would accuse him of negative speech when he wrote words such as the 88th Psalm, a prayer for help in a time of despondency. Nonetheless, he understood that he did not have to stay in that place of discouragement and so he repeatedly called out to God for Divine intervention in his circumstances, and in so doing, two traits stand out:

1. He understood that his role was one of worshipful obedience. David was fully convinced that as long as he had a right view of his Sovereign God his circumstances would be disposed.

2. He invariably included lyrics of thanksgiving for His deeds among the people of bygone generations. Today's generation quite understandably seeks to separate itself from us as far as possible. Why? What mighty deeds has the Lord wrought through the hands of our recent generations of a magnitude such that our children would be inspired to compose songs in celebration and memorial? Even better, let's make the question more personal. What mighty testimony has the Lord worked in *your* life through *your* surrendered and obedient hand that is worthy of song? None, you say? No, not true. If you are a saved, born-again Christian then He has indeed done great and mighty works! The question then becomes, what have you done with your testimony? Who has heard your testimony of His grace and mercy?

Today's music lives in the moment, with little regard for the past and rarely a mention of the future. Is that not what today's education, media, philosophy, and even Christian teaching conveys? Live in the moment. True, Jesus Himself taught that we are not to *be anxious* about tomorrow, but when the reality of eternal life in His presence dropped out of our vocabulary, so did the accompanying reverential fear. The consequences of our failure to tell the kids about life eternal has had far-reaching consequences for we all will live forever; only the destination remains to be seen.

This examination has absolutely nothing to do with the type of music employed in the worship of the church today. There will always be a generation gap in that respect, but if our worship hinges upon having the right external prompting (i.e., the right music), then our worship is misdirected. Personally, I love the very, very old hymns with *"Come Thou Fount of Every Blessing"* at the top of my personal favorites list. As you might imagine, it has been a very, very, very long time since I have heard my preference in open church. If my children, grandchildren, and great-grandchildren were forced to sing hymns of my liking, their ears would bleed and their eyes would likely roll backward in their head. No, it is not about music style, but about how the music of each generation reflects our view of God and it would behoove older generations to stop criticizing our young people and begin to pay attention to the needs of this and upcoming generations before it is too late.

Our narrow examination of this particular altar stone has covered only four evidences: lackadaisical church attendance, lack of commitment to a local church, failure to teach our children, and the absence of recognition of the awe of God as it is reflected in our music. It certainly is not all-encompassing but it has given witness to the need for change and the ones who must change are those of us who are in leadership positions now.

Reverential fear restrains us.

The long history of idolatry has set the stage for some of mankind's most abased moments and often reached tragically comical levels, such as the narrative given in "The Travels of Marco Polo, the Venetian" where we read a colorful account of the lifestyle of a certain society then known to occupy a particular island. The citizens of the island were known to administer worship to the first thing to catch his or her attention each morning, and so on any given day the potential object of their worship was limitless.

How unbelievably sad and yet we can easily fall prey to similar belief systems. Without a reverential awe of God, what is to prevent us from continuing in habitual sin? What else would constrain us from deliberate disobedience? The gracious love of God calls us to communion with Him as we speak words of prayer and praise, but it is the reverential awe which compels us to seek Him even when our flesh rebels and cries out for satisfaction. When nothing else restrains us from rebellion and discord in our homes, it is the reverential fear of God – properly comprehended and taught - which stands between us and the violence of separation. It is this beautiful awareness of a sovereign God that will speak to souls who have a mind to forsake faithful church attendance or those who walk willy-nilly in and out of services, taking sacraments casually and without examination. It is the absence of this reverential fear which offers up our local assemblies as a breeding ground for all manner of sin and infidelities without conviction or accountability. And how can anyone who subscribes to the whole counsel of our God speak evil of one of His other children? The sad commentary is that this paragraph had to be written at all.

The end approaches.

Last, but certainly not least, an appreciation of His might and power will cause us to teach our children to watch in these last days for there is an end approaching.

The undergirding of our faith is this: We serve the one true God. There is no other.

> *Exodus 15:11, "¹¹Who is like unto thee, O LORD, among the gods? who is like thee, glorious in holiness, fearful in praises, doing wonders?"*

If we fail to portray Him to the next generation in this reverential light then how can they believe that He is able to save them?

> *Hebrews 7:24-27, "²⁴But He, because He continues forever, has an unchangeable priesthood. ²⁵Therefore He is also able*

to save to the uttermost those who come to God through Him, since He always lives to make intercession for them. ²⁶For such a High Priest was fitting for us, who is holy, harmless, undefiled, separate from sinners, and has become higher than the heavens; ²⁷who does not need daily, as those high priests, to offer up sacrifices, first for His own sins and then for the people's, for this He did once for all when He offered up Himself."

How can they believe that He is able to keep them?

2nd Timothy 1:12-13, "¹²For the which cause I also suffer these things: nevertheless I am not ashamed: for I know whom I have believed, and am persuaded that he is able to keep that which I have committed unto him against that day. ¹³Hold fast the form of sound words, which thou hast heard of me, in faith and love which is in Christ Jesus."

How can they believe that He is able to deliver them? I saw a bumper sticker once that was so simple and yet insightful it has stayed with me many years. It said, "God loves you and there's nothing you can do about it." What a great truth so aptly stated. Likewise, this first altar stone is so simple that a child can grasp it and so profound that it has perplexed man to this day: How can a God described as "terrible" extend grace to sinful man? Those who heard of His great deeds responded as Rahab spoke to the spies:

Joshua 2:9-10, "⁹ And she said unto the men, I know that the LORD hath given you the land, and that your terror is fallen upon us, and that all the inhabitants of the land faint because of you. ¹⁰For we have heard how the LORD dried up the water of the Red sea for you, when ye came out of Egypt; and what ye did unto the two kings of the

Amorites, that were on the other side Jordan, Sihon and Og, whom ye utterly destroyed."

Grace can only be comprehended when viewed with an awareness of His terror-inducing capacity and the fierceness of His wrath so wondrously appeased by grace through the blood of the Lamb. Self-indulgence will not abide where that full comprehension exists. Indifference will no longer be an issue at hand. When that fullness of who He was and is and ever shall be is made clear, then our grandchildren and great-grandchildren and generations to come can sing with a new, previously unknown conviction:

Amazing grace, how sweet the sound
That saved a wretch like me.
I once was lost but now am found,
'Twas blind but now I see.

CHAPTER 4

STONE NO. 2: SALVATION

As we negotiate this path of life, we are prone from time to time to review the trail behind us and ask (rhetorically of course for we absolutely do not want to hear the answer) what we have accomplished in life. What will our footprint on this earth be once we have stepped into eternity? What kind of an impact have we had, if indeed we have had a noticeable impact? Too much looking backward can put us in a head-on collision with the present, but an occasional reassessment is not a bad thing. Take for instance your walk as a Christian. What has your impact been?

People have come to me on many occasions thanking me for the way the Lord has been able to change their circumstance, life, and environment as a result of some message, a certain teaching, ministry time, or a simple smile. It is reasonable to expect that to be true, but how about those times when your act or your voice seems to be unheralded? One particular instance stands out in my mind. Many years ago my life was in a shambles in every respect. I cannot even begin to describe for you the mess I had made out of my life and every time I went into the house of God I would begin to weep and weep. There was no other place to turn, no one who cared for my soul, but when I walked through the door of that little church on Sunday morning I found relief in tears. Over the next few years God's grace was poured into my life and my circumstances changed. I eventually moved to another state and moved on with a happy, fulfilling life. Some twenty-five years later I re-visited that little town and had a woman approach me in the grocery store to thank me for those tears. Because of that honest, if less than socially acceptable, expression of love for the Lord she had accepted Jesus into her own life and served the Lord in remarkable ways for the rest of her life. Had she not shared that story, I would have remembered those tears as grief and sorrow but because I gained understanding I now see them as tears of release and triumph.

What would Elijah say?

I believe that is true of Elijah there on Mount Carmel as well. He certainly had a fair degree of comprehension of the immediate impact of that event, but I am pretty sure he did not know you and I would be talking about him thousands of years later, examining and critiquing his every action. It is a certainty that he underestimated the long-range impact of his actions for he was honed in on setting the stage for a manifestation of the power of God right there, right then. He knew that before the power of God could be revealed, certain matters must be set in order. Likewise, preparation must be made within the church of America before the power of God can be revealed on a continual and consistent basis, thereby addressing our two underlying thoughts:

Is the Church in America largely ineffective today because of the depraved state of our society?

Or is our society in that corrupt state because the Church is largely ineffective?

So far Elijah's display had been pretty uninspiring. Who wants to travel a long distance (not willingly, but under mandate) to watch a guy stack a bunch of rocks? Do not forget that the people were not there of their own volition; they had been summoned to the mountain by the king. They were happy with the way things were until Elijah started rocking their religious boat, very much like the church in America today.

> *Revelation 3:15-19. "[15]I know thy works, that thou art neither cold nor hot: I would thou wert cold or hot. [16]So then because thou art lukewarm, and neither cold nor hot, I will spue thee out of my mouth. [17]Because thou sayest, I am rich, and increased with goods, and have need of nothing; and knowest not that thou art <u>wretched</u>, and <u>miserable</u>, and <u>poor</u>, and <u>blind</u>, and <u>naked</u>: [18]I counsel thee to buy of me gold tried in the fire, that thou mayest be rich; and white raiment, that thou mayest be clothed, and that the shame of thy nakedness do not appear; and anoint thine eyes with eyesalve, that thou mayest see. [19]As many as I love, I rebuke and chasten: be zealous therefore, and repent."*

Ah, lukewarmness

Have you ever stopped to consider how wonderful lukewarmness can actually be? No, really, it is. Just ask the church in America. Nobody demands anything when you live in that state. You come, you go. You do your perfunctory duty on Sunday morning, offering lukewarm handshakes and smiling lukewarm smiles. You don't even have to feign enthusiasm for the things of the Lord, no zeal. The now renowned "Payday Someday" message by Dr. R. G. Lee, called the church back to reality for failure to follow after the Lord always results in drawing wages in funny money, counterfeit currency.

The deceptive ease and comfort of lukewarmness has hoodwinked us all. America has enjoyed the favor and blessing of God during its lifetime, but that place of blessing and favor in the natural realm has been allowed to walk right into the church, contaminating the purity of our dependence upon Him. The description of the Laodicean church should send chills down our spines. Let's examine those five descriptive words a little closer:

1. *Wretched:* Their greater fault was not that they were wretched but that they were so deluded that they did not *know* they were wretched. "The word signifies being worn out and fatigued with grievous labors, as they who labor in a stone quarry, or are condemned to the mines."[30] So, instead of being children of God, as they supposed, and infallible heirs of the kingdom, they were, in the sight of God, in the condition of the most abject slaves.[31]

2. *Miserable:* Something, or in this case some*one*, whose very presence is as disgraceful and pathetic as to be pitiable. This great church, so rich and prosperous in its own eyes, was an object of derision on the part of those who watched. Those who observe us today must find it puzzling that we devote so much time trying to figure out how to act like them. Disgraceful, pathetic and pitiable.

3. *Poor:* This word does describe one who is poor in the truest sense of the word but it also carries with it the idea of being helpless to change his circumstance, flailing and floundering with no remedy. If that is not bad enough, add to that definition that this poor man had once been in a lucrative, productive place but by his own hand had fallen from that place. He cannot change his circumstance on his own power.

4. *Blind:* This does not describe someone who has no physical sight. Instead, we have here a description of a church that had become so high-minded and lifted up with pride as to be blinded by the smoke of its own arrogance.

5. *Naked:* Naked of spiritual clothing, that is, the imputed righteousness of faith.[32] This church had unwittingly put on the works of their riches as evidence of their righteousness.

To the world we proclaim, "Look at us. This is what God offers you through Christ Jesus. Come and be a part of this wretched, miserable, poor, blind, and naked group!" And then we marvel that they don't come. Have we completely taken leave of our senses?

Real fire or only smoke?

Over the years, the Lord has given me many opportunities to go out into communities in outreach and the first of many hard lessons I learned was this: The world can spot a phony in a heartbeat. They have had all the skullduggery they care to see from people who want to build a congregation so that they can say they have the biggest church in the city. There is no more tolerance for people who arrive to "help" them, only to watch them tuck tail and run at the first sign of opposition. The United States of America is overrun with people with very real needs and the church offers them entertainment. Families are falling apart, our children are being raised by strangers and our men and women no longer even know who they are, and the best we have to offer them is a class on how to force God's hand in prosperity? Seriously?

When I was young, our little farm sported a huge dinner bell mounted on a high pole with a cord which draped down within reach of most adult hands. I was far from being an adult and I have never been accused of being athletic so it took a good deal of leaping to reach the cord but one day I finally managed to ring that clanking bell. I thought it was great fun until neighbors began to pull into the barnyard ready to fight a fire. My mother taught me clearly and painfully that day that you do not ring the bell unless you actually have a fire. The church of America has been ringing the bell for decades now, declaring that revival has arrived and that a move of God is afoot but when respondents walk through the sanctuary doors they find not fire but a sad imitation of the majestic, glorious power of God. When 9/11 brought all America to its knees, masses of former churchgoers and the lost alike flocked to our churches in search of hope, a refuge in the time of trouble, but what they found was the same cold, lifeless religion that they had shunned all along. Despite our bell-ringing, nothing had changed. Indeed it had worsened. And they left again.

The lost world looks longingly to the horizon for hope from some quarter, but the church in America has failed to answer the call in large part because we have been hoodwinked into believing that bank accounts and possessions bring hope. Why, even the lost know that is not true. Our coffers are full; our buildings impressive. We are increased with goods, and yet across the nation our pastors lie prostrate before God seeking something that money cannot buy: a revelation of His glorious presence and a demonstration of His power. Does God not hear the prayer of those blessed men and women? Will He not respond in power? Will He not manifest His glorious presence in such a way as to address our two questions? Or is it possible that we, like Elijah, first need to make preparation for His presence?

The people on Mount Carmel were not wowed by the way Elijah stacked the stones as he repaired the altar. In their spiritual condition; they likely looked upon this whole scene as a disruption of their normal lives. They were unwittingly living out the definition of wretched which we studied out of the Book of Revelation. They were in such deplorable spiritual condition that they could not even recognize the need for correction.

No matter. The re-building of the altar was not for their benefit anyway other than to portray the power of the unity of the twelve tribes of the nation. Elijah had no interest in grandstanding to impress man. He had an audience of One. It was that One who, seeing the proper preparation, was able to respond in explosive power before the people. It was Jehovah God who would change the hearts and minds of Israel, and changing the heart and mind pretty well sums up the challenge we face today. We do things in the church because that is what we do and God help the man or woman who seeks to make changes.

The Holy Spirit beckons.

We might view Elijah's altar as an Old Testament portrayal of today's altar call, which by the way, is almost extinct. That call was a national one while ours lovingly beckons to the individual; that call spoke to a nation living under the Law while ours reaches out with grace and mercy. Nonetheless, the comparison is valid.

Whatever happened to the altar call anyway? Many pastors have completely abandoned the call for salvations in open church, while others admirably persist even in the face of anticipated lack of response. God bless those pastors who persist in faith believing for a return. One could speculate that the open church call to salvation began to diminish as the world view of the church at large began to respond unfavorably to our stance on social issues of the day. Or we could suppose that the revisionist version of the Bible no longer required that confession of faith before man. The more pressing premise rests upon the spiritual health of those already within the fold in response to Jesus' own words:

> John 13:35, "[35] By this shall all men know that ye are my disciples, if ye have love one to another."

The world could care less about our stance on social issues, and the requirement for salvation through the atoning sacrifice of the Lamb of God is not up for re-interpretation, but when the world actually sees the church in America practicing this one commandment of love, then broken and wounded people will gravitate toward her, and fruitful altar calls will become a natural outgrowth.

Now comes the tricky part, tricky because it is going to take a slight, but quite irritating paradigm shift so stay with me.

A change in thinking.

Go back with me to Elijah, if you will. We have already established that the Lord was not compelled to respond to a challenge from the prophets of Baal for the sake of one-upmanship there on Mount Carmel. The very idea is contemptible. So what was His motive? It is always safe to allow Scripture to interpret Scripture and so let's consider once again that oft-quoted passage in 2nd Chronicles 7:14, but this time we will include the verse leading up to it:

> 2nd Chronicles 7:13, "13 If I shut up heaven that there be no rain, or if I command the locusts to devour the land, or if I send pestilence among my people;"

"If I…" the Lord says. In fact three times He said, "If I…" The drought which had plagued the land during the reign of Ahab was divinely ordered (1st Kings 17:1), and the only way that drought was going to end was when He said it was going to end. He is, after all, God. Now, we can more fully appreciate our old friend, Verse 14:

> 2nd Chronicles 7:14, "14 If my people, which are called by my name, shall humble themselves, and pray, and seek my face, and turn from their wicked ways; then will I hear from heaven, and will forgive their sin, and will heal their land."

The coming of natural rain fell squarely on the shoulders of God's people, just as the coming of spiritual rain in these last days rests upon the obedience of the church under the gracious leading of the Holy Spirit. Note the order:

1. Elijah, a man of God, submitted himself to the Lord as He prepared Elijah far in advance of this day of Mount Carmel. He was willing to be trained.

2. He summoned God's people to come near to him.

3. He was sensitive to the right way to approach God. Regardless of what the culture around him said, Elijah knew there was but one way.

4. He saw that the right way had been neglected and perverted and he set about to restore proper approach as he re-built the dilapidated, abandoned altar.

5. Elijah was acutely aware that the events on that mount had nothing to do with him. He did not feel compelled to call the media to cover this event; he brought no attention to himself at all, except as a beneficiary of the covenant of Abraham (1st Kings 18:36).

6. He eschewed all glory, choosing instead to keep the eyes and ears of the witnesses keenly directed toward Jehovah God.

7. Elijah resisted the urge to indulge in self-aggrandizing prayer, so fondly practiced today in hopes of impressing the hearer. His was a very simple prayer, giving glory where glory was due.

8. The purpose is clearly stated in Verse 37, "*…that this people may know that You are the Lord God, and that You have turned their hearts back to You again.*" Oh my, what a glorious day it will be when those words can be clearly spoken over the church in America!

9. Sure enough, when the people saw the undisputable power of God that day, they fell on their faces (a right response when one comprehends true reverential fear) and they called out, "*The Lord, He is God! The Lord, He is God!*"

That was the altar call of Elijah. A man of God spent time with God until He heard the voice of God on the matter. Only then did he speak to the people. He refused to compromise by substituting tolerance for truth; he remained humble, giving God every ounce of glory. He was transparent in his prayer and his heart was broken for his fellow countrymen. He did not seek a following; he did not aspire to some elevated status among the prophets nor did he seek world renown to validate his call; then the power of God fell and people repented.

The altar call in open church only came into use in recent decades. Those close to its birth could address the thought process far better than I, but it would seem that its benefits are far-reaching. For instance, the pastor now knew for certain that this individual had made a commitment to the Lord and he could direct his efforts toward discipleship, a noble intent for certain. It also allows the congregation to see that a child has been born into the kingdom who will need their support and fellowship as they grow in Christ. Laudable indeed. No doubt the primary motivation was to provide a platform for the new convert:

> *Romans 10:9-10, "⁹ That if thou shalt confess with thy mouth the Lord Jesus, and shalt believe in thine heart that God hath raised him from the dead, thou shalt be saved. ¹⁰ For with the heart man believeth unto righteousness; and with the mouth confession is made unto salvation."*

Who has met the requirements of this passage? The person who answers an altar call and confesses before a pastor and a building full of Christians that they have accepted Christ? Or is it the person who makes a quiet heartfelt decision in the pews and then goes quietly out and from that day forth confessing Christ as Lord to their family, friends, and everyday peers?

An absurd question, of course. The salvation transacted in the front seat of the family car is as valid as the one witnessed by hundreds in the most elaborate sanctuary, and the Holy Spirit is very capable of drawing both into the sacraments and corporate worship. Which brings us to the question: Why discuss altar calls at all? It needs to be addressed because at some point in our corporate church past, somebody forgot to teach the kids about the need for salvation.

Count the cost.

The preaching of the unassailable "one way" truth became unpopular and those who persisted in its propagation became ostracized, first by society and later by the church at large. Those men who stood boldly preaching the inevitability of eternal life, either in the sweet presence of the Lord or in a torturous hell have been denigrated, belittled, and written off and shunned as unlearned, placed on par with those who handle snakes and drink Kool-Aid. This abandonment of the need for salvation got a real foothold in the fertile soils of the 1960's when rebellion and self-gratification ruled the stage. Those young people – of which I am one – grew up and married and had families. Salvation by the blood of the Lamb crashed against the shores of self-will and the seaside dwellers reasoned in their hearts that surely a loving God would not send them to hell. Somewhere in their past they vaguely recalled grandparents who spoke of such things, but they were old, after all, and out of touch. If there were such places as heaven and hell, surely their parents would have told them, and even if they had failed to do so then surely their pastor would have warned them. Right?

Self-rule screamed out against submission to a holy God. Beautiful phrases such as "born again" and "saved" began to drop out of our collective vocabulary. Many (and perhaps most) of our seminaries began to produce men and women who were little more than life coaches, teaching Christians how to employ Biblical principles to beat the world system and prosper in this lifetime, rarely if ever mentioning sin, salvation, or eternal life.

Jesus spoke a parable in the Gospel of Luke that our leaders would do well to pass along. Allow me to bring that parable into today's world. It seems that there was a very wealthy man whose business began to prosper in greater and greater measure and his wealth multiplied unbelievably. He already had a mansion with a filled five-car garage in the suburbs of Atlanta, a seaside home in Aruba, and a luxury yacht at his disposal. What could he buy with this new influx of dollars, he wondered? He thought and thought and finally it dawned on him: nothing. He could do nothing; he could build greater investments and then just sit back, take his ease, eat, drink, and be merry.

Luke 12:20-21, "²⁰But God said unto him, Thou fool, this night thy soul shall be required of thee: then whose shall those things be, which thou hast provided? ²¹ So is he that layeth up treasure for himself, and is not rich toward God."

America is a hard place to win souls. It is. But we need not blame the world for that. It is you and it is me.

Within a year of my ordination I heard that a Billy Graham sponsored crusade was coming to town. Unfortunately, I had more zeal than I did sense, and in my naivete, I marked my calendar for the first organizational meeting. Could not wait. We were going to win souls together; we were going to work in unity. Wow! The day of the meeting finally came and I rushed to the host church. A number of pastors and associates were already there milling around the room while examining some of the literature provided by crusade coordinators, and then I heard it begin: the grumbles, the questions. They went something like this: "How do I know for sure I am going to get my fair share of the converts?" "Why does he get to be first in line?" "Why does he get to have more altar workers than I do?" You get the picture. I was devastated. I could not stop crying. My cluelessness had run headlong into reality and it was a painful collision.

Take that attitude; advance it about three decades, and that, my friend, pretty well sums up the state of salvations in America in recent decades. It is only by the grace of God that we see salvations at all in this environment, but we have not crossed the finish line yet, brothers and sisters. Contrary to what satan would have us believe, the race is still in progress so jump up, dust yourself off, and run. There is much yet to be accomplished!

Viable, sustainable revival.

Great men and women of God have been praying for revival for decades. This coveted spiritual renewal cannot be one of a flash-in-the-pan variety, but a viable, sustainable one. It has been a long while coming, but it is now time to suspend our exhausting busyness, fall to our knees, and review what we know for certain:

1. We know for certain that it is not His will that anyone should perish. Any. None.

   1ˢᵗ Timothy 2:4-6, "⁴Who will have all men to be saved, and to come unto the knowledge of the truth. ⁵For there is one God, and one mediator between God and men, the man Christ Jesus; ⁶Who gave himself a ransom for all, to be testified in due time."

   How is it possible that we have become so hardened to the eternal destiny of those around us? Can we assign that indifference to a lack of reverential fear? Or did somebody forget to teach decades of children of the reality of eternity?

2. We know for certain that salvation belongs to *"whosoever believeth in him should not perish, but have everlasting life." (John 3:16)*

   Unapologetic, unwavering certainty that Christ is the solitary door to eternal life is a highly unpopular belief today, most assigning it as nothing more than an arguable hypothesis. To those of us who know it to be truth, it is enigmatic to listen to pluralists who love to debate that, as though reaching a variant conclusion could somehow negate Christ's provision on the cross. Ah, the arrogance of Babel is alive and well.

3. We know for certain that He commissioned us to become fishers of men. The power-packed gospel, faithfully ministered by the power of the Holy Spirit has been rendered as a series of lifeless, earthbound pragmatic teachings, leaving the lost to agree with the Apostle Paul:

1ˢᵗ Corinthians 15:19, "¹⁹ If in this life only we have hope in Christ, we are of all men most miserable."

In Paul's day there were men who taught emphatically and persuasively that there is no resurrection from the dead, no eternal life. These men were easily identifiable, openly espousing their opposition to the teachings of the followers of Christ. Those who advocate that belief today are around every corner veiled by their particular field of study. Since the world controls most of our media outlets, both electronic and print, we are all touched in some measure by deceptive teachings every day in very subtle, almost imperceptible ways. Television, movies, and even documentaries offer up a virtual menu of eternal options:

a. There is no such thing as eternal life. A lie.

Hebrews 9:27-28, ²⁷And as it is appointed unto men once to die, but after this the judgment: ²⁸So Christ was once offered to bear the sins of many; and unto them that look for him shall he appear the second time without sin unto salvation."

b. There is eternal life, but God would never send anyone to hell. That one is true. It is man's own choice.

2ⁿᵈ Peter 3:9-10, "⁹The Lord is not slack concerning his promise, as some men count slackness; but is longsuffering to us-ward, not willing that any should perish, but that all should come to repentance. ¹⁰But the day of the Lord will come as a thief in the night; in the which the heavens shall pass away with a great noise, and the elements shall melt with fervent heat, the earth also and the works that are therein shall be burned up."

c. We will come back again and again in search of that elusive state of enlightenment.

1ˢᵗ Thessalonians 4:14, "¹⁴ For if we believe that Jesus died and rose again, even so God will bring with Him those who sleep in Jesus."

This particular menu item is widely accepted in America today due in part to its popularity among notable, trusted celebrities. Some of today's most remarkable, memorable music extols the virtues of reincarnation in seductive fashion, extending a voice of comfort and assurance that we need not worry about an all- powerful God and eternal destinations. We are, they assure us, just a part of the circle of life.

Make no mistake, dear friend, there is no endless round of life. Wonderful movies, breathtaking musical compositions, but fiction. We get one lifetime to make eternal choices.

4. We know for certain that our beloved Saviour awaits us with glorious anticipation.

John 17:24, "²⁴ Father, I desire that they also whom You gave Me may be with Me where I am, that they may behold My glory which You have given Me; for You loved Me before the foundation of the world."

Here is where our natural vocabulary falls short. Can you even envision such grandeur of glory? Can your ears even hope to comprehend the refrains of worship inhabiting and dominating that atmosphere? How can we hope to grasp the words *"may be with Me where I am..."*? Maybe it would help if we looked backward in time to events which have already transpired. For instance, what do you suppose was going on in heaven when the Lord purposed to breathe life into the nostrils of this nuisance creature called man? Do you suppose that the citizens of heaven took no note? Do you imagine that they were unaware of the eternal bearing of this one moment? We can only postulate of course, but inside of what we do know about His dwelling place we can be very certain this was not the case. Heaven must have been intensely engaged that day just as the atmosphere must have vibrated with divine passion when heaven's emissary appeared to the shepherds in the fields crying out, *"For there is born to you this day in the city of David a Savior, who is Christ the Lord. And this will be the sign to you: You will find a Babe wrapped in swaddling cloths, lying in a manger."*³³ And as if that were not enough, that angel was joined by back-up singers consisting of a *"multitude of the heavenly host"*.

Can you feel the excitement of the audience of heaven as those words were spoken? Can you sense the pulsating anticipation of what had just been set in motion? Now can you get a little better idea of what it will be like when the desire of Christ Jesus Himself has been fulfilled and we are where He is, dwelling with Him, never ever to be separated from His presence again?

*2nd Timothy 2:11, "¹¹It is a faithful saying: For if we be
dead with him, we shall also live with him:"*

How is it possible that we – having possessed such unspeakable
promises – stubbornly refuse to tell others of salvation, even those that
we love more than life itself? How can we turn an indifferent shoulder
to those who are in danger of eternal destruction? Slightly over 150,000
people die on planet earth every day, day in and day out. Only the Lord
knows how many of those 150,000 have accepted Christ; only the Lord
knows how many have heard and rejected, and only He knows how
many never heard the gospel at all because, yes, somebody forgot to
tell somebody.

The church in America has listened to and gladly embraced a lie,
one which offered immediate gratification. Over the past fifty years,
we have become the personification of the church of Laodicea, and
like that Revelation church, we have become so wretched we do not
care. We have preferred the teaching of the superiority of this life and
its pitiable, perishable attractions over the unutterable glories of His
presence. Small wonder, for that lie was birthed and promoted by the
one who *"transforms himself into an angel of light,"*[34] and as is his habit,
he took pre-existing truth and salted it with just enough perversion to
distract us and cause us to take our eyes off the prize.

*Philippians 3:13-14, "¹³Brethren, I count not myself to
have apprehended: but this one thing I do, forgetting those
things which are behind, and reaching forth unto those
things which are before, ¹⁴I press toward the mark for the
prize of the high calling of God in Christ Jesus."*

Cheating at solitaire.

I once knew a woman who played solitaire by the hour. Her deck of
cards (for this was pre-computers) was worn and faded but that did not

matter. She would sit at the kitchen table patiently dealing out hand after hand, strategically placing those cards in descending order. If practice made perfect, she must have been quite good at the game, but sometimes when she was stymied by a move she would look all around to make sure no one was looking, re-locate a problem card or two, and take off again, consistently ending up with four piles of perfectly formed stacks. And she apparently felt a sense of accomplishment.

Like this woman, we have been cheating at solitaire. As the church is made up of many members of one body, the responsibility and accountability for witnessing of the gospel is incumbent upon each of us. Generations gone by spread the cards on the table, but when the going got tough and soul-winning became unpopular they simply looked around, rearranged His commission and placed it in the stack, quickly concealed from sight by other, more enticing, teachings. The following generations (including and maybe especially my own) have buried that salvation card progressively deeper in the pile to the end that evangelistic efforts, effective altar calls, and even the most rudimentary consciousness of witnessing has nearly vanished.

Can we stem the tide? I married a sailor at a very young age who was stationed aboard a U. S. Navy aircraft carrier, a massive floating city as it were. When it was approaching the day for a return to port, we wives would clean and launder, wax the car, visit the beauty shop, and make preparation for the return of our men; then we waited. The enormity of that ship required it to steam ever so slowly into port. Families gathered on the dock, most toting picnic baskets and coolers, waiting impatiently as the ship's motion slowed to a near standstill, its movement almost imperceptible. And we waited. Tugboats steamed out of port to meet the gray giant, only its towering radar gear visible on the horizon. It took the better part of an entire day for the ship to pull alongside and lower the gangplank. No one could speed up that process. You just cannot turn a 900-plus foot hunk of steel on a dime. By the same token, we will not change the course of the church in America by making an announcement. It is going to require change at the most basic level, steering this ship in a new direction. It will require brutal self-examination on the part of her leaders and a refusal to fail. "Not in the clamor of the crowded street. Not in the shouts and plaudits of the throng, but in ourselves, are triumph and defeat." (Longfellow)

We are in this for the long haul.

> *1ˢᵗ Peter 3:13-16, "If with heart and soul, you're doing good, do you think you can be stopped? Even if you suffer for it, you're still better off. Don't give the opposition a second thought. Through thick and thin, keep your hearts at attention, in adoration before Christ, Your Master. Be ready to speak up and tell anyone who asks why you're living the way you are, and always with the utmost courtesy. Keep a clear conscience before God so that when people throw mud at you, none of it will stick. They'll end up realizing that they're the ones who need a bath."[35]*

This version of that passage makes our charge admirably clear: When occasion arises be ready to be a witness, that being one who testifies as to what they have seen, heard, or experienced. *"Let the redeemed of the Lord say so.[36]"* If you have experienced the healing hand of God in your body, heart, or mind, say so. You now have access to peace and rest in your spirit; say so, and then wait on the Lord. Their response is not your responsibility for it is His harvest; witnessing, however, is yours.

We talked earlier of the "Payday Someday" sermon. In that message, Dr. Lee spoke beautifully of heavenly crowns, one of which is reserved for those who win souls.

> *Philippians 4:1, "¹Therefore, my brethren dearly beloved and longed for, my joy and crown, so stand fast in the Lord, my dearly beloved."*

> *1ˢᵗ Thessalonians 2:19-20, "¹⁹For what is our hope, or joy, or crown of rejoicing? Are not even ye in the presence of*

*our Lord Jesus Christ at his coming? [20] For ye are our glory
and joy."*

Nothing within the limits of our comprehension can compare
to the glory of looking around heaven some day and seeing those to
whom we have witnessed. Sometimes we sow, sometimes we nourish,
sometimes we water, and, yes, sometimes we reap, but whatever your
role, joy unspeakable will fill your heart when you see them safely in
His presence.

By sleight of hand our solitaire player was doomed to bogus reward
as are we when we settle for religious rites rather than obedience. The
negligence and disregard of this particular altar stone has brought
counterfeit gratification, but the promise is to us of a crown of joy to
offer at the feet of Jesus. How sad it would be to have none to cast.

Tomorrow's atmosphere.

It is a strange thing, actually. While this grand powerhouse of beauty,
the very body of Christ, has been distracted by trinkets and baubles,
our children are incredibly focused on the heavy things of this life.
Their future holds unprecedented moral and ethical challenges, their
approach to their world will require forward-thinking innovation, and
very little of that society will be based upon the old thinking that we
hold so dear. These kids are smart and resilient. They are world-wise in
ways we cannot even fathom, and they are bright enough to know that
there are some things us old folks have failed to teach them. They know
something is missing; they just do not understand what it is.

Let's resolve to change that. We have the answer to fill the void
in their ever searching hearts. Tell them that there is an answer to
loneliness. Tell them that there is a cure for the emptiness in their hearts.
Tell them that there is a safe haven for them when their earthly family
is shattered. Speak to them of a bright hope for tomorrow and a divine

friend who will dispel the dark and smothering blanket of loneliness and isolation.

> Jeremiah 5:22, "²²Fear ye not me? saith the LORD: will ye not tremble at my presence, which have placed the sand for the bound of the sea by a perpetual decree, that it cannot pass it: and though the waves thereof toss themselves, yet can they not prevail; though they roar, yet can they not pass over it?"

No man has ever even come close to comprehending the magnitude of the grace of God, either in its scale or in its weight or worth. The closest analogy that I can conceive of is to picture grace as the five oceans of the earth (Arctic, Atlantic, Pacific, Indian, Southern (or Antarctic)). They say that 70.9% of the earth's surface is covered by water; only 29.1% is land. That is enormous and yet it is not infinite. It is measurable. Some smart guy somewhere could figure the precise mass of the earth covered by dry land and the mass covered by water and compute just exactly how much water covers this earth. Not so with grace. It is immeasurable, infinite. God will never run short of grace, and so when you watch the evening news and it all sounds hopeless and when the kids' music makes you blush and their tattoos and piercings make your heart palpitate, remember this: your sin was just as great as theirs. That bears repeating: your sin was just as great as theirs. Yes it was. But someone told you about Jesus and you have never been the same. Our kids deserve no less.

CHAPTER 5

STONE NO. 3: THE WORD OF GOD

Thus far we have carefully placed two stones: The first was reverential fear of God; the second, a return to a consciousness of the need for salvation. With those two securely in place, it is time to roll the third stone into position, which is the teaching of the Word of God.

This stone differs in its character from the previous two in this way: Man can choose whether he will fear God; it is his prerogative. Man can choose to be saved or not; it is his decision to make. However, with no respect to man's stance, the Word of God endures endlessly.

1. It is untouchable. Emperors and kings have tried to stomp it out, atheists have tried to discredit it, humanists have demeaned it, and our own educational system and political leaders have tried to legislate its demise. Governments come and go, rulers rise and fall, but the Word of God prevails. The Word of God cannot be separated from the very divine personage of God, and no man can change that.

    Isaiah 40:8, "⁸The grass withers, the flower fades, but the word of our God stands forever."

2. The Word was in the beginning.

   Hebrews 11:3, "³Through faith we understand that the worlds were framed by the word of God, so that things which are seen were not made of things which do appear."

   There has never been a time when the Word was not operational. That's an elusive concept for those of us who insist on strapping timepieces on our wrists. Nonetheless it is true.

3. The Word is evident in the end.

   Revelation 19:11-13, "¹¹And I saw heaven opened, and behold a white horse; and he that sat upon him was called Faithful and True, and in righteousness he doth judge and make war. ¹²His eyes were as a flame of fire, and on his head were many crowns; and he had a name written, that no man knew, but he himself. ¹³And he was clothed with a vesture dipped in blood: and his name is called The Word of God."

   The end is not yet and so we are not inclined to ascribe immediate significance to many of the prophetic words, consigning them to some imprecise tomorrow. However, our Christian walk is made more stable and constant when we make some effort to comprehend the end of things.

4. The Word is unchangeable.

   Hebrews 13:8, "⁸Jesus Christ is the same yesterday, today, and forever."

   John 8:58, "⁵⁸Jesus said to them, 'Most assuredly I say to you, before Abraham was, I AM.'"

5. The Word is our sole source of truth:

Psalms 119:142, "[142]*Thy righteousness is an everlasting righteousness, and thy law is the truth."*

The battle for the Bible.

In the days of the Roman Empire few men had access to copies of the Gospels. Even then, Roman officials came to see that the suppression of Christianity demanded the destruction of the Scriptures, and so the last great persecution of Christians included the burning of the Scriptures.[37] Christians were presented with a critical dilemma. Their closely-held commission to spread the gospel could no longer be precisely accomplished since Scripture was the only true source of teaching.

The Bible, as breathed to man by the Holy Spirit, is a powerful force. Oppressive governments historically embark upon two initial acts toward their subjects:

1. *Banning all assemblies.* Satan fears the church when we come together in unity. Things begin to happen when we join hearts and hands and pray in faith. Mountains move, rivers are redirected, and most remarkable of all, hearts are changed.

2. *Banishing all Bibles.* Tyrant after tyrant has tried to hurl the Word of God out of existence and out of the spirit of man like the iconic shot put athlete. What foolish arrogance. Time after time we read testimonies of the hatred and violence directed toward the Word of God and any man or woman who is courageous enough to take a stand for its proliferation. Those oppressive governments seem to be more concerned about the Bibles in the hands of their people than they do about earthly weapons. There is no more powerful weapon than the Bible.

Remember our analogy of the con man mesmerizing his audience with one hand while the other busily performed the swindle? Same principle. The familiar observation that the Bible is the best-selling book of all time obscures a more startling fact: The Bible is the best-selling book of the year, every year. No one tracks exactly how many Bibles are sold each year in the United States, but a conservative estimate puts it in excess of 25,000,000 Bibles, of countless translations and versions. Statistically speaking, those who define themselves as consistent Bible readers sport 3.6 copies of the Bible. I'm not sure how someone ends up with that .6 copy, but I am pretty sure I heard a guy preach from it one time.

The arrival of the newspaper marked one of the big events of the day when I was a kid. It was a scant publication by today's standards, filled with new recipes, exciting tidbits about who had visited who, who was in the hospital (pre-HIPAA), and who had given birth. It made for a whole lot more interesting reading than today's newspaper by the way, and it was absolutely stress-free. None of that mattered to me. I just wanted the funny paper and a good wad of silly putty. I could press that gray goo down, peel it off and magically turn Nancy into Twiggy or Dagwood into a giraffe. With a quick pull or twist I could distort and disfigure that print, altering the original intent. Such is the case with the handling of God's Word today.

An old story is told which brings some light to the criticality of adhering to the Word as given: A woman touring in Europe cabled her husband: "Have found wonderful bracelet. Price seventy-five thousand dollars. May I buy it?" The husband promptly cabled back, "No, price too high." Unfortunately, the cable operator neglected to insert the comma and so the woman received a positive message which read, "No price too high." She immediately went out and bought the bracelet, but her enjoyment of the piece was short lived because the husband quickly realized that a little error can have far-reaching implications. This lighthearted story illustrates a weighty truth: The Scriptures must be respected, revered, and handled with care for the Bible is our only certain source of truth.

As valid as this line of thought may be, it is not the objective of this particular altar stone. I defer to scholars and theologians far beyond my reach. Instead, it is an exhortation to return to and restore the very existence of teaching in local churches.

The Word was held tightly in times gone by, doled systematically and strategically from the elevated platform. A particular Scripture or passage was read, expounded in acceptable measure, and the Book was closed. This became the norm, of course, because of the absence of printed material. The average man simply did not have access to the printed Word, and the Word in its purest form was their only source.

We have no such defense. The Word is readily available, and yet very few are teaching it. Pastors across this nation stand in the pulpit every Sunday morning, preaching the Word of God with all their heart. They understand that the people that they serve will need that message in the coming week. When the congregation crosses the threshold after services, they will be stepping out into a society steeped in sin and perversion. Seductive images will call out to them from the racks in supermarkets and drug stores in the quest for the minds of believers as they seek to re-define what is normal. Movies are almost incomprehensible in their lewdness, vulgarity, and perversion. Even pre-school children will cross that threshold on Sunday morning out of the pastor's reach and into a society that seeks to destroy them. It is estimated that the average American was exposed to about five hundred advertising messages per day in the 1970's; that figure has now skyrocketed to over five-thousand per day. The sub-conscious mind of our children will continue to be bombarded with conflicting images and messages not only in spiritual matters, but in physical, familial, societal, intellectual, professional, and economic arenas as well. With what yardstick will they measure right and wrong, good and evil?

Today's pastor finds himself mired in a perpetual cycle of defensive teachings. Sunday evening services were once a backstop for basic Bible teachings but those have largely been abandoned among even the most traditional congregations. There is no hard data to tell us why that's true, but let's consider two of the more likely contributing factors: The pastor got tired because the people quit coming and the people quit coming because the pastor got tired.

Those are broad statements and likely overly simplified, but I think most will agree it is pretty accurate. And we haven't even mentioned the nearly defunct operation we fondly knew as Sunday School. Oh my goodness, my goodness, fellow Christians, what have we done?

The incumbency belongs first upon the shoulders of fivefold ministers:

> *Ephesians 4:11, "¹¹ And He Himself gave some to be apostles, some prophets, some evangelists, and some pastors and teachers."*

We are the ones with the commission and we are the first ones accountable to God:

> *Ephesians 4:12-16, "¹² for the equipping of the saints for the work of ministry, for the edifying of the body of Christ, ¹³ till we all come to the unity of the faith, and of the knowledge of the Son of God, to a perfect man, to the measure of the stature of the fullness of Christ; ¹⁴ that we should no longer be children, tossed to and fro and carried about with every wind of doctrine, by the trickery of men, in the cunning craftiness of deceitful plotting, ¹⁵ but speaking the truth in love, may grow up in all things into Him who is the head – Christ – ¹⁶ from whom the whole body, joined and knit together by what every joint supplies, according to the effective working by which every part does it share, causes growth of the body for the edifying of itself in love."*

Our identity crisis

Can we take a lesson from nature? Our back yard serves as home to several squirrels, one of which we have even named Johnny Bench because every day at precisely 3:45 he climbs up on our limestone bench and entertains us with his antics. Fascinating creatures, these. Their agility is unbelievable and their bravado no less inspiring. These long-tailed wonders take death-defying leaps from power lines to trees to fence tops and back again with ease. They hang upside down on our towering oak trees, just out of reach of the family dogs, chattering and mocking, and occasionally I am pretty sure they are just showing off. What do you suppose would happen if one of those rodents arbitrarily decided to act like a turtle? What if he elected to take on an identity that was not his to take? His poorly conceived scheme would result in great frustration and even peril. One can only imagine what his evasive maneuvers might look like. Turtles have a lot going for them, but lateral dexterity is not one of them. Likewise, much of the church has attempted to morph into an entertainment center in order to hold the sheep in the fold and to entice more sheep to come in. We have tried to out-world the world, and to what end?

1. The unwavering truths of the Bible have been conceded for the sake of earthly approval, rendering the absolutes of His Word powerless in the lives of the hearers, because *"faith cometh by hearing, and hearing by the word of God."*[38]

   Hebrews 11:6, "⁶But without faith it is impossible to please him: for he that cometh to God must believe that he is, and that he is a rewarder of them that diligently seek him."

2. More and more of our children are wandering away from their spiritual roots. A recent newspaper headline announced, "Religion losing some appeal." One young twenty year old

woman expressed herself this way, "I feel like people can believe what they want to believe without having to follow rules."[39]

Similar studies in the past have directed their attention to Catholicism, Protestantism, as well as other less populous groups, but a new identity emerged dominant through this new study: the Nones, or those who refute any and all faith affiliation or labels. The Nones are now the second largest category after Catholics. Of those results, Albert Mohler, president of the Southern Baptist Theological Seminary in Louisville said, "This is a wake-up call. We have an incredible challenge ahead for committed Christians."

The numbers are alarming enough, but perhaps even more disturbing were some of the side notes to the original study. For instance, one in four of those surveyed say they believe in astrology and reincarnation, and 58% say they feel 'a deep connection' with nature and the earth.

That our children are searching for something is obvious.

   a. The average age for first experimentation with alcohol
       is now 12; for drugs, 13.

   b. Over half of the kids who graduate from high school
       will have experimented with drugs and 33% will have
       tried drugs other than marijuana.

   c. Nearly 1 in 16 will have tried cocaine.

   d. Suicide is the third leading cause of death in young
       people aged 15 to 24; the fourth leading cause of death
       for children between the ages of 10 and 14. Even more

shocking is that for every completed suicide, twenty-five have attempted and failed.

"Attitudes and values of the adolescent and preadolescent have shifted away from authority figures and toward more pleasure-seeking, big-money, fast-living people – toward sex, drugs, alcohol, and money."[40]

Who is to blame? Who forgot to tell these precious babies that God is a sovereign ruler who consults no man? Who forgot to tell these young men and women that the Word of God is absolute authority and that their eternal destination is not multiple choice? Who forgot to tell these children that God has a plan for their lives? And, for goodness sake, who forgot to tell the kids that God loves them and that His love is totally unconditional?

Who is responsible for this atrocity? We are. We did it. As leaders, we have walked away from our responsibility to teach the Word of God to our babies. We forgot to start when they were born teaching them of the goodness and the omnipotence of God, and every generation that passed found this neglect a little easier with less and less conviction. We join generations gone by as we are now forced to acknowledge that we have sown to the wind and are now reaping the whirlwind.[41]

Sheep droppings

Bear with me, fivefold minister, for this really is a word of edification and exhortation. Now we turn to the responsibility borne by the sheep. The people of God are behaving like…. well, like a bunch of sheep.

Matthew 9:35-36, "³⁵ Then Jesus went about all the cities and villages, teaching in their synagogues, preaching the gospel of the kingdom, and healing every sickness and every disease among the people. ³⁶ But when He saw the multitudes, He was moved with compassion for them, because they were weary and scattered, like sheep having no shepherd."

The word weary is actually better stated as harassed. Sheep without proper shepherding are subject to harassment which results in bewilderment, restlessness, a sense of hopelessness, and agitation. Harassed sheep are not able to lie down and rest and their relationship to other sheep is disrupted by mistrust and fears. Does this sound like anyone you know? Sheep need a shepherd. That being said, even our animal kingdom namesake has the good sense to drink water and graze to remain alive and healthy.

We are all familiar with the old "you can bring a horse to water", right? Surely we can assign the same proverb to sheep? I love this olde version: "A man maie well bring a horse to the water, But he can not make him drinke without he will." Or how about this version: "Who can give water to the horse that will not drink of its own accord?"

The point at hand is this: It is the responsibility of the leaders of the church to make sound teaching available to the people; it is the responsibility of the people to avail themselves of the teaching and to pursue the Word of God on their own.

In its most basic approach, our secular education methodology establishes certain knowledge and skills as building blocks. We would not attempt to teach classical literature to a class of children who cannot read. Common sense tells us that we should not expect advanced math skills from a second grader, and yet we have not applied that same common sense approach in our Bible teachings. Somewhere out there are teachers of children, hundreds, maybe thousands, gifted by the Lord in elementary classroom instruction. Where are you teachers? Our kids are waiting for you. Stand up. Innovate. Create. Construct systematic curriculum. Take them to the next level where the teachers of pre-teens can take over. Youth leader, connect with the teachings of the elementary classes and develop those teens as you prepare them to bridge over to the young adult stage.

Slippery slopes

One of my favorite people in the whole world is my own mentor in the everyday workings of ministry, Pastor Rebekah Ryan. No book, no lecture or theologian could have taught me more about true ministry than Sister Becky, as she is known east of the Mississippi. At eighty-three years of age, she continues to walk out the ministry established by her husband many years ago and she does so with panache and style, love and compassion, and the spiritual strength of an Olympic grappler. I like to think that her late husband, Dr. Jack Ryan, must surely be cheering her on from the balcony of heaven, as he often described his destination. Grappling aside, Sister Becky does have a quality conspicuously absent among ministers today: she has a sense of humor. Two of my granddaughters once spent the night with her, her granddaughters, and several other friends at her log cabin home in the hills of southern Indiana. Sister Becky has a whole repertoire of entertaining ideas and so this white-headed dynamo took the girls out to a long steep slope, sprayed water the entire length and then went back to the top and dumped a bottle of liquid laundry detergent, sending it flowing to the bottom. With a short run and shrieks of unbelief, these oh-so-off-the-runway girls shot down that hill again and again, coming up caked with wet red clay.

I thought of that evening just now because of that long, steep slippery slope. Our failure to teach the whole Word of God in recent generations has stationed us right on the precipice of a spiritual slippery slope. Our lackadaisical approach to the teaching of the Word of God must be stemmed. Our kids and their kids are in grave danger in America if we fail.

Consider Mount Carmel once again. Do you think the outcome there would have been a different story had Elijah approached the event haphazardly? What if Elijah had decided it was too much trouble to gather all those Israelites in one spot? That act alone required a herculean effort, you know. What if he had reversed the order and offered up a prayer seeking the evidential power of God without making proper preparation? Would the fire have fallen anyway? Would the improperly prepared sacrifice have been consumed? Would the Lord have somehow excused Elijah's carelessness simply because He loved him?

Christian leaders are crying out for revival across America; they are on their face before God repeatedly, seeking that manifestation of His mighty power. However, we must ask ourselves this question: Have we tied His hands because we have not made proper preparation? Are we hindering His response?

Dear pastors, history will record that you served in one of the toughest spiritual times and environments known to mankind and you are to be commended because you continue to stand strong. Your prayers have been heard and your cries have rung out through the heavenlies. Humble yourself before Him. Get back to basics. Examine your own heart, your own motives, your agendas. Examination begins at the top.

> Psalms 139:23-24, "²³Search me, O God, and know my heart: try me, and know my anxieties: ²⁴And see if there is any wicked way in me, and lead me in the way everlasting."

Calling all teachers

My prayer for you over the altar stone of the Word is that you will begin to see potential teachers in your congregations, people who have the gift of teaching. It is one thing to have knowledge and stand before people in the name of teaching, but it is quite another to have the gift of teaching. Gifted teachers can transport people right into the Bible.

Characters become as real as their own neighbors, and the hearer learns to feel the breath of their words and the texture of their clothing. Teachers can convey the brutality of war and allow the listener to eavesdrop on the broken hearts of those left behind. They can help the student understand the smell of sweat and blood of the battle hanging in the air. Why even the begats become enthralling under the voice of an anointed teacher.

Not all pastors are teachers. Let me repeat that: Not all pastors are teachers. I know that is not a popular statement but it is true and it is one that I hope you will consider. You cannot do it all. You simply cannot. You cannot teach Sunday School, preach Sunday morning and evening services, and preside over mid-week services (which, by the way are also nearly extinct). Begin to pray that God will raise up teachers among your sheep who will be able to effectively communicate the Word of God, and then invest yourself in the training and preparation of that one or two. If you already have that person(s) in the house, then release them in their work. At some point you have to trust someone.

If you are one of those gifted teachers, then stand up! What are you waiting for? If you believe that you are a teacher by gifting, sit down with your pastor and start a dialogue. That is number one on the "to do" list for you. Make certain that you are in tune with your pastor and the vision of the house. Next, pursue studies. If that means you need to burn the midnight oil, do it. Your pastor may have some really good suggestions or even a list of recommended courses. Prepare yourself before you stand up to teach; you cannot teach what you do not know. You will be held accountable by the Lord Himself for what you teach so take your time and study, study, study, and make proper preparation. When you *and* your pastor agree that you are ready, that the time is right, and the venue is open, then teach with all your heart.

Work alongside your pastor to develop and implement a systematic approach to Bible study. A methodical approach to study should begin in the nursery and follow a defined order through adulthood, always building knowledge and avoiding the storybook fashion of random stories. By the time the elementary boys and girls become adults under such a system, they should be well-balanced, thoroughly equipped in the whole counsel of God.

> *Acts 20:26-28, "²⁶ Wherefore I take you to record this day, that I am pure from the blood of all men. ²⁷ For I have not shunned to declare unto you all the counsel of God. ²⁸ Take heed therefore unto yourselves, and to all the flock, over which the Holy Ghost hath made you overseers, to feed the church of God, which he hath purchased with his own blood."*

Resist the urge to entertain while entertaining the urge to provoke interest. Use technology. Use (tried and true) available materials. Do not feel compelled to re-invent the wheel. Invest yourself in your students. Pray over them and their families.

And to the precious, cherished sheep

My last charge on the altar stone of the Word is to the sheep.....it is time to wake up. The water is going to be brought to you, but only you can make the decision to drink. The pastor and teachers can study and study and work and prepare, but *"Who can give water to the horse that will not drink of its own accord?"*

I love Indiana University basketball. GO HOOSIERS! But don't you know that sometimes they play when I need to be at the church? Bummer. Let me speak right into your heart, oh sheeply folks. Show up for every Bible teaching opportunity that is offered at your church. Avail yourself of every opportunity to learn the Word of God. Luxuriate in it. Memorize it. Exercise it.

The hand of the Lord will respond to a heart which is attentive to Him, to obedience, and to mountain-moving faith so let us restore the Word of God to its place of prominence as the axis around which every activity revolves. Study it. Teach it. Preach it. Apply it. Keep it ever before the eyes of the people.

These are exciting times we live in. Who knows but what some day, people will shout out, "It was never seen like this in America!"[42] Step into the place of blessing with our brother Job:

Job 42:12, "Now the Lord blessed the latter days of Job more than his beginning….."

STONE NUMBER 4: CONSECRATION

God is a God of order. From eternity past to eternity future, the plan of God steadily unfurls, reality converging with faith just beyond the horizon. Most of what we see and experience in that reality of life flaunts itself in the face of that truth, but it is true nonetheless. He has never faltered from His ultimate plan. He began with a man in the Garden, a man with whom He could walk and talk and commune; He partnered with that man, granting *"dominion over the fish of the sea, over the birds of the air, and over the cattle, over all the earth and over every creeping thing that creeps on the earth."*[43] (Did you ever wonder what grand limitations God might have set upon Adam's comprehension of Himself had man *not* fallen?) His plan never truly concludes, never meets that horizon, but so far as this earth is concerned it ends with a spiritual populace washed in the blood of the Lamb, prepared to dwell as worshipers in His presence forever without end.

God's penchant for order is evident in the strategic placement of our previous three altar stones. Each stone carries its own independent message to be sure, but the back story here can be found in their interdependency. When our perception of God (<u>reverential fear</u>) fails to include His might and His power, then the criticality of <u>salvation</u> becomes a moot point, optional at best. Thus began America's slippery slope. Having relegated the great I AM to a companion role alongside other wannabe gods invented by man, all inducement and incentive to study the Bible as <u>the Word of God</u> has been negated. It is that "many ways to God" idea which has caused us to be content with a thirty minute message on Sunday morning, hand fed by someone standing behind a pulpit. Under that belief system, the individual Christian can only hope that man is preaching truth because there is no personal knowledge with which to test it.

'Tis a very fine line indeed, the distinction between a legalistic faith and one which demands humility and the sacrifice of one's own will. That line became a very divisive one in the spiritual life of America during the last few decades. In a sincere intent to revel in the marvel of His amazing grace, the idea of any cost to the believer was chipped away, little slip by little slip.

During the days of the ghastly reign of Hitler, Dietrich Bonhoeffer, marveling at the passive stance assumed by the church, wrote of man's grasp of grace in three manifestations which he had observed:

1. Cheap grace, that "going to church and hearing that God just loves and forgives everyone, so it doesn't really matter much how you live"

2. Legalistic grace, "that God loves you because you have pulled yourself together and are trying to live a good, disciplined life" in your own strength.

3. Costly grace, "that we are saved, not by anything we do, but by grace."[44]

Costly idolatry

Do you see what has happened since we began to neglect that very first stone some fifty years ago? We now live in an idolatrous nation. Listen to the Word of the Lord as given through the Prophet Jeremiah:

Jeremiah 2:5, "⁵thus says the Lord: 'What injustice have your fathers found in me, that they have gone far from me, have followed idols, and have become idolaters?"

It is a rhetorical question, of course, for God is a perfectly just ruler and judge and injustice could never be found at His throne. The question is posed to reveal the heart of man. Why would men turn their backs on a compassionate and loving God whose mercies are new every morning and turn instead to worship dead idols? The level of self-degradation and humiliation involved in the worship of idols is far beyond imagination. Both secular history and the Bible record for us scenes of the most extreme debauchery and even speak to us of parents who offered up their own children in an effort to appease these counterfeit gods and goddesses.

The historical diaries of the travels of Marco Polo tell the story of a particular region of the world where idolatry reigned supreme and where parents dedicated their newborn daughters to the indulgence of idols. The baby girls were prepared and groomed for the service of idol worship and then as soon as they reached a suitable (and apparently negotiable) age, then they would begin to participate in the feasts. Dead, lifeless images were elevated to the place of a god, honored and revered. The banquet was spread (although the honoree did not eat much) while the young girls performed vulgar and coarse dances, all to induce favor from this powerless, feeble hunk of matter.

The brand of idolatry practiced by those Israelites on Mount Carmel was of a different variety, of course, but their antics to please the idols were no less preposterous, cutting themselves until "*blood gushed out on them*"[45]. For worship of that cruelly demanding idol the people had refused the hand of a God whose mercy knows no end? The Israelites who gathered around that altar were not much better. How did they get so far away from truth? They had allowed themselves to be seduced by the society around them little slip by little slip. It did not happen overnight; their downfall crept into the camp gradually, one compromise at a time, that same process which ensnares mankind yet today. It crawled along almost imperceptibly.

Are we really so different from these Israelites? Decades ago the sanctity of Sunday mornings was violated, and family worship time stood teetering on the height of that slippery slope. That (undefinable) generation of parents still retained the knowledge of proper worship and Biblical service to the Lord, but their consciousness of the fear of God had begun to fade. Parents began to stay in their pajamas on Sunday morning or work overtime or do something sporty, but not all was lost. They carefully dressed up the kids and put them on a bus or a van, relegating the spiritual development of their children to complete strangers, and then they crawled back into bed, went fishing, or began preparing the grill for the Sunday afternoon football party. A generation or two earlier that would have been unthinkable, an abomination; a few generations later, we think it admirable that parents should care so much as to drop their kids off at the front door of the church.

Let's not lose sight of our original pursuit. Our quest in this altar stone journey is not so much to pinpoint culprits as to examine evidence of the veracity of the charges. In the case of this particular stone it could be summed up thus: over a period of time man's self-dependence soared while dependence upon One True God declined. And therein lays one clue to our mystery:

Is the Church in America largely ineffective today because of the depraved state of our society?

Or is our society in that corrupt state because the Church is largely ineffective?

If you were to ask someone from the 1950's generation how they came to know Jesus, most would tell you that it was during Sunday School or under the direct influence of some wonderful, faithful teacher.

Is it any wonder that the enemy of God fought so hard to kill Sunday School? Without proper teaching of the absolute truths of the Bible:

> *Judges 17:6, "⁶In those days there was no king in Israel, but every man did that which was right in his own eyes."*

It was also around those tables and in those classrooms where Christians of all ages learned of consecration, a word seldom heard in the churches of America today.

As with all the other stones, this is not intended to be a deep treatise of theology, but a simple word of exhortation to the church. Nonetheless in order to get a clear view of the principle of consecration we must back up to the Old Testament where the act of consecration finds its root.

> *Exodus 30:30, "³⁰And thou shalt anoint Aaron and his sons, and consecrate them, that they may minister unto me in the priest's office."*

Consecration then and now

We all know that to consecrate means to make or to declare sacred; to set apart or dedicate to the service of God; or to devote or dedicate to a specific purpose. By the way, I cannot pass up the opportunity to read on into the next verse: *"³¹ And thou shalt speak unto the children of Israel, saying, This shall be an holy anointing oil unto me throughout your generations."*

Aaron and his sons were set apart, designated by God to fill the priestly office. No other authority or power in heaven or on earth was capable of making such an appointment. Aaron and his descendants were chosen by God without dispute; no man was consulted and no man could dispute the appointment. Some tried and the result was catastrophic.⁴⁶ These chosen few were consecrated or set apart and dedicated to the exclusive service of Jehovah God.

This act of consecration did not confer upon Aaron and his descendants any semblance of perfection. When Aaron got out of bed the morning after his consecration ceremony, the mirror over his vanity still reflected the same old guy; no halo or wings. He probably still had onion breath from the previous evening's meal and he still had to comb the tangles out of his long, coarse hair. He still had to deal with the obligations of a family man, and you know how grueling that can be. He still sweated in the heat of the day and sometimes he had to stop and clean out the sand from his sandals. To the visible eye, nothing had changed; he was still very much man but in truth, nothing would ever be the same because he was now the man set apart, chosen by God for a specific destiny and for a perfect work and service. From that day forward Aaron's wants and desires were secondary to that of God. He had been consecrated, set apart for the Lord.

John 3:30, "³⁰ He must increase, but I must decrease."

Though a New Testament Scripture, it precisely describes the transaction between God and Aaron at the time of consecration. As the High Priest of Israel, he was *"appointed for men in things pertaining to God, that he may offer both gifts and sacrifices for sins."*[47] The earthly high priest was subject to weakness and because of this he had to offer sacrifices for himself as well as the people.

> *1ˢᵗ Peter 2:9, "⁹ But ye are a chosen generation, a royal priesthood, an holy nation, a peculiar people; that ye should shew forth the praises of him who hath called you out of darkness into his marvellous light:"*

Chosen? By whom? Jesus made it clear that He specifically chose the twelve disciples,[48] even the one who was a devil. What about us? How can we relate?

Each of us became a part of that chosen generation and royal priesthood when we accepted Christ's great salvation. Each of us should remember that day. I remember it clearly. I was young; I did not comprehend all that was about to flood into my life. Words like consecration were foreign to me and so, in effect, I was consecrated before I grasped consecration. I only knew that I was a sinner who desperately needed to be saved and I knew that Jesus had made a way of redemption. I just wanted to follow Jesus. Then slowly but surely teachers began to build my understanding, speaking words of commitment and consecration, both in Sunday School and from the pulpit, and a whole universe of Christian living began to open up to me. I could only understand as a twelve-year-old would, that His will was more important than my own. The Lord's Prayer took on new light, *"Thy kingdom come, Thy will be done on earth as it is in heaven."*[49]

That was eons ago, in the mid '50's. Things were different then. Families were mostly intact and actually talked to each other. When Dad and Mom and all six of us kids walked through the sanctuary doors on Sunday morning we (unwittingly) knew that the message we were about to hear would verify and confirm the message we had seen and heard in our home all week. We did not stop to think about that, of course, but that was the principle at work.

What about today's generation? Where do we expect them to learn the truth of consecration, of being set apart to Him in love and in devotion and in service? How do we suppose they will know what it means to die to oneself? Who will tell them that there is a cross to be borne? It is rarely taught in open church, and when it is offered it is so intertwined with self-exaltation that the concept of sacrificial service is hidden from view. The confused and perplexed state of the family in America hinders the Bible's intent for teachings in the home; yet we have the audacity to criticize our younger folks because they fail to meet our expectation for commitment to their faith.

> *Mark 10:21, "²¹ Then Jesus beholding him loved him, and said unto him, One thing thou lackest: go thy way, sell whatsoever thou hast, and give to the poor, and thou shalt*

have treasure in heaven: and come, take up the cross, and follow me."

This verse is taken from the story of the rich young ruler who came running after Jesus to ask the question, *"…..what shall I do that I may inherit eternal life?"* He already knew the commandments and had done his very best to keep them since his youth; he was looking for an easy answer. Jesus looked lovingly upon the heart of that man and saw that he lacked one thing: a willingness to die to self.

> *Romans 6:3-7, "³ Know ye not, that so many of us as were baptized into Jesus Christ were baptized into his death? ⁴ Therefore we are buried with him by baptism into death: that like as Christ was raised up from the dead by the glory of the Father, even so we also should walk in newness of life. ⁵ For if we have been planted together in the likeness of his death, we shall be also in the likeness of his resurrection: ⁶ Knowing this, that our old man is crucified with him, that the body of sin might be destroyed, that henceforth we should not serve sin. ⁷ For he that is dead is freed from sin."*

That rich young ruler bears a striking resemblance to much of America today, racing to identify themselves with His name (over 51% of Americans call themselves Christians), but reticent to identify with His cross. The knowledge of self-denial and consecration has been tucked away safely out of view in the apron of the church.

Tozer gave us seven revealing categories of self-examination, helpful in evaluating our own comprehension of consecration:

1. *What is it that we want the most?* This is an ongoing test, one that is administered moment by moment and one that I recently failed miserably. We had been considering the purchase of a new home. Each of us wrote down the particular features we would like to have in that home and tucked those slips of paper

safely away in our Bibles as an act of faith in the Lord and His promises. A few days later in my prayer time the Lord impressed upon me the need to remove my piece of paper and read it through. I did so and put it back. This went on for a few days (I am a slow student) and then one morning it finally hit me. I wadded that piece of paper up and wrote a new one which read, "Whatever you want, Lord." I still carry that piece of paper in my Bible as a reminder of His preeminence.

2.   *What is it that we think about the most?* There was a time when people lived in near isolation, absent transportation, and unscathed by media. By contrast, consider how few hours per day your mind can be at rest now, unmolested by the screams of technology and society. Very few. So does being set apart mean that our minds must continually and consciously consider the Lord? What are we supposed to do with all those other cerebral bombardments? I once heard a preacher on the radio describe it like this: Let's suppose that you have a personal problem that must be dealt with. You get up in the morning and go to work as usual, but that problem is in the back of your mind. You may successfully perform a hundred different tasks that day, speak with a number of co-workers, and even go out for a bite to eat at lunch time, but the consciousness of that issue remains in the back of your mind. So it is with the Lord. Behind all the demands of each day, there should be a sure awareness of His presence through the precious Holy Spirit. Always there. Always comforting. Always speaking. Always reassuring. That's a benefit of a consecrated life.

3.   *How do we spend our money?* The rich young ruler did not go away from Jesus grieving because he had great possessions, but because the comfort, prestige, and power his possessions yielded meant more to him than eternal life. Sight vs. faith. He chose sight and that caused him to grieve. I wonder whether that man

ever truly enjoyed his wealth after that day or if his pleasure was forever tainted by Jesus' piercing words.

4. *How do we spend our leisure time?* We are created beings: body, soul, and spirit, and all three need nourishment. A well-rounded, consecrated Christian is free to enjoy a healthy leisure life with gusto, knowing full well that his life is rightly surrendered. It seems that Americans have fewer leisure hours than ever before, but opinion does not match up with the facts. According to the Bureau of Labor Statistics, 95% of Americans aged 15 and older devote over five hours per day to leisure activities (5.8 hours for men; 5.2 hours for women). The figure dropped for those in the age bracket of 25 to 44, with only 4.2 hours per day.[50] Since I have not had 5.2 hours of daily leisure time available in years, I want to know who got my share, don't you?

5. *Who do we like to spend time with?* Again we find an area where formal teaching has nearly crumbled through the generations. There was a time when the local church was a place where believers found a safe refuge and a place of acceptance and love among fellow believers. Hospitality was the norm. There was a common bond among those people that could not be found anywhere else and so when the Sunday fellowship dinner or meeting on the grounds arrived, not only did the entire congregation show up but they brought extended family and neighbors to join in. Even passersby were known to stop for a bite and conversation and boy did we have a time!

The friendships formed in those local churches extended far into the day-to-day life of the believer. Children enjoyed the company of other Christian children and bonds formed which lasted a lifetime.

Another part of that socialization was the care and nurturing of the pastor. Nary a Sunday went by but the pastor and his family found themselves honored and embraced, seated around a host table being treated to the best food that the host family could afford. In retrospect, I am pretty sure that the pastor and his family would have rather been home hanging out on the couch, but by these acts of sacrificial warmth on the part of the host and the guest, the pastor got to know the family; he had an opportunity to observe the dynamic of that family; he was better able to gauge the needs of his parishioners; and a personal relationship slowly developed that could not be bound under any other circumstances. Around that table children were taught how to respect God's man and his family. As he blessed the food we children comprehended that this man did not know *about* God; he knew God. He became the model of consecration for a whole family over a plate of Mom's home fried chicken.

6. *Who and what do we admire?* Who are our heroes? Are they Christian? Who is it that warrants our admiration? Do their lives reflect attitudes of self-denial and consecration? Or do we make allowances?

7. *What makes us laugh?* This thought is not a clean joke vs. off-color joke issue at all. Instead, ask it from the vantage point of what it is that brings you joyful laughter? The Bible is a clear advocate of laughter and joy:

Proverbs 15:13, "¹³ A merry heart maketh a cheerful countenance...."

Even in its charge to be sober and vigilant, the Bible commissions us with the fullness of joy.

1ˢᵗ *Peter 1:8, "⁸ Whom having not seen, ye love; in whom, though now ye see him not, yet believing, ye rejoice with joy unspeakable and full of glory:"*

Science and the Bible agree on the benefits of laughter and so the question is not whether we should laugh but what is it that triggers laughter in our life? Where does our heart find mirth?

My parents always loved to visit other like-minded churches when we were young. Dad and Mom would walk in and try to be as inconspicuous as you can be with six children following on your heels, but when you have that many kids bunched up together, something is bound to go wrong. You can just bank on it. I especially remember one such Sunday when we visited a tiny little country church not far away. My parents were punctual to a fault, but on this particular Sunday we ran a little bit late. We spilled out of the car (starched petticoats and all) and as quiet as a litter of church mice we tiptoed up the big limestone slab steps, when Daddy suddenly realized that they were in the midst of the opening prayer and in those days nobody but nobody moved during prayer time. He turned around real quick and "shhhd" us kids, and when Daddy said "shh" you "shhd." We could clearly hear the man inside lifting his voice up to the Lord as he fervently prayed "for those just outside the church doors." Six kids nearly fell down the steps laughing and there was no stopping us. One would gain control and five others would burst out again. For the life of me I could not tell you whether we ever went in or if we left. All I remember is the wonderful laughter.

The demise of the teaching of consecration

We who are older can almost trace with personal recollections the vanishing of the teaching of consecration in open church. As with all of our other neglected and decayed altar stones it did not happen overnight, but through decades of decline.

Once again, we turn to music as an evidence of our pursuit. For instance, forty to fifty years ago, a Sunday morning service in America's local churches began with one certain, identifiable move: the inevitable reach for the hymnal. There is another word from the past. Most of today's younger generations have never held hymnals in their hands so for the sake of clarity, let's review: With those hymnals (generally tattered and dog-eared) we could sing along even if we had never heard that particular piece of music, and trust me, they were oh so necessary because those old hymns were painfully wordy.

I randomly pulled a typical example of my many old hymnals off the bookshelf just now and discovered some twenty-six hymns dedicated to the topic of consecration. When was the last time you sang songs of consecration?

> *All to Jesus I surrender, All to Him I freely give;*
> *I will ever love and trust Him, In His presence daily live.*
> *All to Jesus I surrender, Make me, Saviour, wholly Thine;*
> *Let me feel the Holy Spirit, Truly know that Thou art mine.*
> *I surrender all, I surrender all.*
> *All to Thee, my blessed Saviour,*
> *I surrender all.*[51]

Truly, brothers and sisters, this is *not* a campaign to get back to the old music; there is some fabulous worship music available today. Nor is it meant to put the hymnals back in the pews (which are mostly gone now anyway). It is an attempt to examine the evidence to substantiate or dispel the charge and then access every avenue available to us to prepare our kids for the challenges they are facing and will face. There is no better way than through the universal language of music.

> *Colossians 3:16, "⁰⁶ Let the word of Christ dwell in you*
> *richly in all wisdom; teaching and admonishing one*

*another in psalms and hymns and spiritual songs, singing
with grace in your hearts to the Lord."*

1. The word "*teach*" in this passage means to instruct by word of
    mouth with the understanding that the teaching offered will
    increase the understanding of the pupil, to the end that the will
    of the hearer would be shaped accordingly.

2. To "*admonish*" means to put into the mind for instruction and
    to warn the hearer, even to the inclusion of reproof.

3. The root word "*songs*" in this verse means to say or to confess.
    "The original use of singing among both believers and idolaters
    was in the confession and praise of the respective gods. Paul
    qualifies it in Colossians 3:16 as spiritual songs in association
    with psalms and hymns because this root word by itself might
    mean any kind of song such as a thought of battle or harvest or
    festival."[52]

I can still hear Daddy's tenor voice ringing out, "*Have thine own
way, Lord. Have thine own way. Thou art the Potter; I am the clay.*"[53] Of
all the hymns I found, however, the following lyrics speak most clearly
to the beauty of consecration, of being set apart unto the Lord:

> Nothing between my soul and the Saviour,
> Naught of this world's delusive dream;
> I have renounced all sinful pleasure,
> Jesus is mine; there's nothing between.
>
> Nothing between, like worldly pleasure,
> Habits of life though harmless they seem,
> Must not my heart from Him e'er sever,
> He is my all; there's nothing between.

Nothing between, like pride or station,
Self or friends shall not intervene,
Tho it may cost me much tribulation,
I am resolved; there's nothing between.

Nothing between, e'en many hard trials,
Tho the whole world against me convene;
Watching with prayer and much self-denial
I triumph at last, with nothing between.[54]

Do you see the teaching and admonishment resident in these lines? They are there, moving the heart of the singer from love to commitment to conviction to confession and back to love.

The ABC's of consecration

Music was not the only source of teaching of consecration in bygone days though. It may be hard to believe but our schools actually used the Bible as a source textbook and a tool in teaching children to read, killing the proverbial two birds with one stone. "A is for Adam, who was the first man. B is for Bethlehem, where Jesus was born. C is for Cain who killed his brother, etc."[55] A child who learned under these unconstrained textbooks would read, "Adam and Eve were happy in Eden as long as they loved God more than they loved to have their own way."[56]

Barring a world-quaking miracle from the throne room of God, our public schools in America will never again be allowed to teach from the Bible as a textbook. The burden of instructing our children in consecration and self-denial now rests squarely upon the family and the local church.

I can hear screams of protest, "This is not the old days!" I hear that protest and I agree wholeheartedly and so did Solomon:

Ecclesiastes 7:10, "¹⁰Do not say, 'Why were the former days better than these?' For you do not inquire wisely concerning this."

Nonetheless, a baseline must be established and our history is the source from which that baseline must be drawn. You and I cannot go backward two or three hundred years for examination for we have no firsthand knowledge of those times other than by reading what that generation left us as a legacy, but by giving life to our collective memory we have a reliable control point for comparison.

And so the objections are heard; it is *not* the way it used to be; it is not even the way it used to be two generations ago. The principle of total surrender of one's life to Christ is completely foreign. The idea of subjugating the will of the individual to the will of God is summarily rejected by most young people today. This is America, the land of the independent spirit. These kids were birthed into a brutal, ferocious anti-Christian culture with little to no comprehension of how it got so bad, and if they cannot grasp how it happened, how can they hope to turn it around? Or even why they should want to turn it around?

There is nothing new under the sun,[57] Solomon wrote. America did not invent corruption and perversion. History is packed with such societies. It is the inevitable state of a nation who turns away from God, but it is incumbent upon us to encourage the emerging generations to stand tall in the Lord, confident in Him. This is no time for the faint of heart. The last days are broadly defined as the time following the ascension of Christ and so we can say with absolute certainty that we are in the last days. We can say with a high degree of conviction that we are in the last of the last days.

Luke 9:23-26, "²³ And he said to them all, If any man will come after me, let him deny himself, and take up his cross daily, and follow me. ²⁴ For whosoever will save his life shall lose it: but whosoever will lose his life for my sake, the same shall save it. ²⁵ For what is a man advantaged, if

he gain the whole world, and lose himself, or be cast away?
²⁶ For whosoever shall be ashamed of me and of my words,
of him shall the Son of man be ashamed, when he shall
come in his own glory, and in his Father's, and of the holy
angels."

Take a good hard look at the teachings available in your local congregation, leaders. Are the principles of consecration taught and encouraged? Are you doing a good job of keeping a balanced message before the sheep? Do you see evidence that the people of your local church comprehend the principle of consecration? If so, then praise God for those wonderful folks. If not, try folding those teachings into your messages, your lessons, and your example.

Self-sacrifice declines; hopelessness on the rise

Here is perhaps an even greater challenge: Look around you at the children of our society as a whole. Take time to see the looks on their faces. Do not criticize, look. See. Sit in a mall sometime for two to three hours and just observe. Take note of the lack of self-respect; note the absence of self-worth. Look at the vacancy in the eyes. Hopelessness cannot be quantified, but despair of the worst variety can be seen on many of those faces, the kind of despair that comes when there is no answer on the horizon, no light at the end of the tunnel.

A dear lady visited our church years ago. No one seemed to know her or how she had come to visit and so as she and I struck up a conversation I invited her to share lunch with me a few days later and, to my surprise, she agreed. Conversation is not a problem for yours truly and so we talked for quite a while but I could not make any inroads into her situation in life. Her answers were friendly, but brief and to the point. Longing to look more deeply into her heart, I asked her this question: "If you could ask the Lord for any one thing and know that you would get it, what would you ask for?" A blank stare was her response. I told you that I was conversational, but obviously not articulate, because my question had left her speechless, and so I re-phrased the question. I even gave her some multiple choice selections: home, furniture, car, clothes, husband? No response, not even a tremor of hope. I made a few runs along this line and finally realized that she had so completely lost hope that she could not conceive of anything so grand ever coming her way. I am not sure that I had ever met someone so completely devoid of hope.

Despair is a terrible disease in our society; in fact, according to most experts, an American takes his or her own life every 13.7 minutes. According to the American Foundation for Suicide Prevention, over 38,000 people died by suicide in the U. S. during the reporting year 2010, placing suicide in tenth place as the leading cause of death for adults and even higher in the order for children and teens. These babies are the most precious of all our national treasures and, folks, they have lost their way, and it is our fault. I know that does not absolve them of all responsibility, but how can they know an endlessly loving and gracious God if no one teaches them or lives a life of mercy before them? How can they observe Christ-likeness when we have neglected our own consecration?

Our kids have little interest in what we say, but they are amazingly tuned in to what we do. For instance, go to a buffet-style restaurant after services next Sunday morning….not to eat but to observe. Ten minutes earlier those folks were standing in the sanctuary dressed in their Sunday best, singing and looking all consecrated and holy, but those buffet bins have the power to resurrect self-will. God help the man or woman who reaches through the line for a ladle of mashed potatoes. You are smiling, aren't you? You have seen it. So have our children. We wear our rotten attitudes for the world to see. Consecration is an internal act, but its presence (or lack thereof) is on open display 24/7.

It is a simple concept really, this dying to self and living unto Christ. You may not know the theology of consecration. You may not be able to give a Webster's definition and you may not be able to quote the Bible on the topic, but deep in your spirit you know it and you know we have let it slide. Our pastors must teach it, our church leaders must reinforce it but dying to self and living unto Christ….that is the responsibility of every Christian. And make no mistake; the kids have eyes on you.

I gave My life for thee, My precious blood I shed,
That thou might'st ransomed be, And quickened from the dead;
I gave, I gave My life for thee, What hast thou given for Me?

My Father's house of light, My glory circled throne
I left for earthly night, For wanderings sad and lone;
I left, I left it all for thee, Hast thou left aught for Me?

I suffered much for thee, More than thy tongue can tell,
Of bitterest agony, To rescue thee from hell;
I've borne, I've borne it all for thee, What hast thou borne for Me?[58]

CHAPTER 6

STONE NUMBER 5: PRAYER

At first it seemed to me that this stone of prayer should be placed right on top of the first, the stone of reverence. It seemed only right that spotlighting the line of communication between the revered one and His people had to be the connecting link for all the other stones. However, the Holy Spirit impressed upon my heart a larger truth. Follow the pattern with me:

1. Reverential fear brings a consciousness of our frailty.

2. His great love puts that fear into perspective, drawing us to Him in salvation.

3. His drawing speaks to us of grace and life, affirmation and reproof; *"growing up unto Him in all things"*[59] through His Word.

4. That sets Christians apart *"that ye may be blameless and harmless, the sons of God, without rebuke, in the midst of a crooked and perverse nation, among whom ye shine as lights in the world."*[60]

5. The progression of these four naturally results in the restoration of assembly prayer.

Once again I sense a need for a brief disclaimer. This is not intended to be an in-depth study of prayer but an exhortation to the church and her leadership to restore its proper place in the corporate life of the people. Clearly, God hears the cry of a sinner calling out for salvation. The honest cry of the heart never goes unheard. Nonetheless, there is a power resident in corporate prayer that goes largely untapped today.

Our pattern is given to us in the Book of Acts.

> *Acts 1:1-2, "¹ The former account* (the Gospel of Luke) *I made, O Theophilus, of all that Jesus began both to do and teach, ² until the day in which He was taken up, after He through the Holy Spirit had given commandments to the apostles whom He had chosen,"*

The Gospel of Luke speaks of the life and ministry of Christ, tracing His birth, childhood, and ministry. In Acts 1:1, "The implication is that what follows in this second volume known to us as Acts describes what Jesus Christ continues to do since his ascension as the Holy Spirit empowered believers to carry on the purposes of Christ. Thus we find the apostles performing miracles, but attributing the cause to Jesus Christ."[61]

We often hear the question posed, "Why do we not see more miracles today?" We certainly do have them among us as we hear testimonies here and there, and we celebrate each and every one, but why not more often? Why not routinely? Why not as the apostles did?

Was it because these men were with Jesus day in and day out? That one cannot stand up to examination because *"…if Christ be in you, the body is dead because of sin; but the Spirit is life because of righteousness."*[62] We have Him with us every second, every minute, every hour of every single day and not only with us but within us. Sure, the disciples walked and talked with Jesus on this earth, up close and personal, but even then they were not that close.

Was it because their commission to the miraculous was greater than ours? Wrong again.

John 14:10-12, "¹⁰Believest thou not that I am in the Father, and the Father in me? the words that I speak unto you I speak not of myself: but the Father that dwelleth in me, he doeth the works. ¹¹ Believe me that I am in the Father, and the Father in me: or else believe me for the very works' sake. ¹²Verily, verily, I say unto you, He that believeth on me, the works that I do shall he do also; and greater works than these shall he do; because I go unto my Father."

In fact, the impetus of our personal faith is under higher demand than that of His own day. Thomas is unduly remembered for his doubt but this brother did us a great favor by helping us to understand our own faith. The disciples were assembled for fear of the Jews so you can imagine the unease that hung in the air of that place. The conversation must have been in hushed, probably somewhat argumentative tones. Had Mary Magdalene really seen the Lord? Had He really spoken to her? How could it be true? They had all witnessed His death and had probably visited the tomb at one point or another. What even greater retribution would they encounter now at the hand of their fellow Jews if the rumor got out that Jesus was alive? And right smack in the middle of their human reasoning, Jesus showed up. Isn't that just the way? He showed them His hands and His side and there was an encounter transacted in that place that we are incapable of fully comprehending. Then He was gone.

As you know Thomas was absent from that gathering. One can only guess what could have been so important as to keep him away. Maybe his mother-in-law came over for dinner. Who knows?

John 20:25, "²⁵The other disciples therefore said unto him, We have seen the Lord...."

Words can be so inadequate. There is no way that the disciples said, "Ho-hum, Thomas. We just saw Jesus." No, no, no. There had to have been incredulous joy and exhilaration and marveling! All that they had believed and hoped for had taken on a blanket of forlorn despair at Calvary. They had been so certain, so full of faith and in one short span of time, their hope had been sucked into a vortex of darkness, but now, with the report of but one witness, their faith and confidence had been re-awakened; their hope had been resurrected. All that Jesus had spoken was alive and well.

We can try to envision the various scenes which may have played out that day, but one thing we know for certain: when Thomas opened that door, he ran headlong into a bunch of revived, radical disciples!

> *"....But he said unto them, Except I shall see in his hands the print of the nails, and put my finger into the print of the nails, and thrust my hand into his side, I will not believe."*

Remember, Jesus was not visibly present for this conversation, but eight short days later as the disciples assembled once again, He appeared and spoke directly to Thomas:

> *John 20:27, "²⁷ Then saith he to Thomas, Reach hither thy finger, and behold my hands; and reach hither thy hand, and thrust it into my side: and be not faithless, but believing."*

Jesus did not condemn Thomas; it was simply a statement of caution. Don't be faithless, Thomas. Don't fall into the company of unbelievers.

Bear with me. There is a reason this story is so important to our prayer stone.

Jesus granted to Thomas precisely what he had spoken, and Thomas made a conscious decision to lay aside his unbelief, to refute his own faithlessness, and he spoke triumphant words of faith, responding loudly, *"My Lord and my God."*[63]

Now listen closely to Jesus' response:

John 20:29, "²⁹ Jesus saith unto him, Thomas, because thou hast seen me, thou hast believed: blessed are they that have not seen, and yet have believed."

You did great, Thomas. You saw and you believed. I acknowledge your faith. However, there are millions and millions of people yet to come who will not have that benefit of sight and yet will believe. Jesus was talking about you and me and, therefore, collectively, the church. We, who came later after His ascension, actually have an advantage because the demand on our faith is greater. That truth is difficult to digest for great faith is most often fostered and nurtured in the most difficult of times. Witness the operation of the church during times of persecution. When great need arises, great faith responds.

A few years ago, I took a fascinating tour of the Raccoon Mountain Hydroelectric Facility near Chattanooga, Tennessee. It is a massive operation through which TVA provides power to distributors, power associations, and consumers. Simply put, water is pumped from the Nickajack Reservoir located at the base of the mountain into the reservoir at the top of Raccoon Mountain during low demand hours. The reservoir covers some five hundred twenty eight acres, forming a massive lake, still and calm and beautiful. When demand is high the water plummets downward through a tunnel drilled in the center of the mountain, driving the generators in the mountain's underground plant, powering homes and industry throughout the region. I can tell you that observing this colossal operation made this woman feel small and overwhelmed.

As individual believers, we operate on much the same basis. During the low demand times of life – those times when all is going well - we accumulate a basin of faith, filled and maintained by prayer. That reservoir is a marvel to behold, calm and serene, but then life inevitably comes along and we find ourselves awash in a period of high usage, those times when the wheels are falling off of everything around us, placing a demand upon that faith reservoir. By faith, the floodgates open and His promises power us through the turbulent waters of life. God loves it when His people live by faith; it pleases Him.

There is absolutely no ground to support a theory that the prayer of the individual believer of our day is any less fervent or passionate, any less fruitful or effective, or any less spiritual than in years gone by. None. There is much evidence, however, that the prayer life of the assembled body of Christ has suffered enormously and it is that shared prayer life which this stone seeks to restore.

Bible based spiritual revival is sustainable.

As Peter preached his message of repentance recorded in Acts Chapter 2, some three thousand souls were added to the church.

> Act 2:42, "*42 And they continued steadfastly in the apostles' doctrine and fellowship, in the breaking of bread, and in prayers.*"

They were devoted to proper teaching, to relationship with other believers, to the observance of communion, and in *prayers*, and from those foundational exercises came people of whom it was said, "*….These who have turned the world upside down have come here too.*"[64]

Could it have been that simple? Could simple faithfulness and obedience to revealed truth really have turned the world upside down? By their acts these men unwittingly provided an answer to the church in America today. Their simplicity of worship testifies that in order for a spiritual awakening to be viable it must be sustainable and that can only be achieved by obedience to the Word through the ministration of the Holy Spirit.

Spiritual awakening or renewal will not come as a result of some program conceived and developed in the heart of man. Our devices, no matter how well intended, are of no value. God will not violate His Word and His Word clearly gives us direction such as this:

James 4:8, "⁸ Draw near to God and He will draw near
to you...."

For once we will not look to the past for our evidence but instead we will shape our proof forward from today by the Word on its own merit:

Leviticus 26:8, "⁸ Five of you shall chase a hundred, and
a hundred of you shall put ten thousand to flight; your
enemies shall fall by the sword before you."

This promise is generally accepted to be one of a proverbial nature, tucked away amid other assurances, great and numerous. Obedience to the Lord's commands carried certain assured benefits and equally assured penalties for disobedience, much as those described in the renowned Deuteronomy 28. Being mortals as we are, we tend to read and remember only the blessings, but there has always been a consequence of neglect.

Consider now three citations taken from the great Song of Moses:

1. *Deuteronomy 32:4, "⁴ He is the Rock, His work is perfect; For*
   all His ways are justice, A God of truth and without injustice;
   Righteous and upright is He."

   As Moses spoke the words of this song in the hearing of the assembly of Israel, he began to review the history of the nation that he loved and he did so with extraordinary candor, stating the faultless omnipotence of the One True God.

2. *Deuteronomy 32:18, "¹⁸ Of the Rock who begot you, you are*
   unmindful, And have forgotten the God who fathered you."

   Moses now began to remind the people of God's great love toward them, having even fathered them as a people (a rare father image to be found in the Old Testament) and chided those who had gone before in that they had become unmindful of Him, careless in their worship.

3. *Deuteronomy 32:30, "³⁰ How could one chase a thousand, And two put ten thousand to flight, Unless their Rock had sold them, And the Lord had surrendered them?"*

    Now we get to the crux of our citations. God had promised His people, *"Five of you shall chase a hundred, and a hundred of you shall put ten thousand to flight; your enemies shall fall by the sword before you."* That was the promise secured by obedience but negated by disobedience. Therefore, since the Israelites had turned their back on God and turned instead to foreign gods the reverse came to pass.

You see, according to this passage (and others) it was virtually impossible for obedient Israelites to be defeated unless God Himself had surrendered them. Conversely, it was impossible for Israel to be victorious without the mighty hand of God.

> *Deuteronomy 32:37, "³⁷ He will say: Where are their gods, The rock in which they sought refuge? ³⁸ Who ate the fat of their sacrifices, And drank the wine of their drink offering? Let them rise and help you, And be your refuge."*

Notice that this time it says "gods." Little g. And "rock." Little r.

Oh my goodness, God loved those people. He loved and He wooed and His heart was broken again and again. It was forever in His heart to do good for His people and they just could not hold it together long enough to receive.

Thank you, Jesus, for grace.

With God all things are possible.

In ways and for reasons we can only hope to comprehend, the one true God, creator of all that was and in and ever shall be, hitched His will to the obedient faith of man. Small wonder then that without faith it is impossible to please Him.[65] Oh what He will work for that one here and there who catches hold of that truth.

Let's bring those Old Testament truths to bear on the New Testament church. Time after time Jesus encouraged His listeners to extend their faith. Remember the water-walking episode when Jesus chided Peter, "*O thou of little faith, wherefore didst thou doubt?*"[66] How about the father seeking help for his son who seized, foamed at the mouth, and gnashed his teeth? The father had a modicum of faith but he made the mistake of putting that right out there in the air by saying, "*If you can….*" to Jesus. Jesus responded, "If you can…." as if to say "I cannot believe you just said that," but He continued, "*…..all things are possible to him who believes.*" To which the father responded "*Lord, I believe; help my unbelief.*"[67]

Faith moves mountains, brings healings, triggers divine miracles, calls lost family and friends to salvation. The boundary of faith filled prayer is without limit. The miraculous is what we should be calling normal! That being the case, why in the world is the church neglecting assembly prayer?

The New Testament makes specific reference to prayer over 160 times, 57 of those references being penned by Luke either in the Gospel or the Book of Acts. In addition, that particular writer was led of the Spirit to place a greater emphasis upon the prayer life of Jesus than the others, speaking of seven specific occasions not found in other Gospels. Ruling out coincidence as a possible reason for that strong emphasis upon prayer, we can conclude that the powerful presence of the Holy Spirit was making clear to the New Testament believer the unchangeable connecting link between faith and prayer and the miraculous.

We can only speculate concerning the diminishing choruses of prayer meetings. The potential causes are endless, but here are a few to feed the spark of your own conclusion:

1. We have entrusted our spiritual articulation to an elite few in our local churches whose voices somehow seem more pious than our own. We perceive that they know the right phrases, quote the right Scripture passages, and say it in words that (we have wrongly been told) the Lord wants to hear. We have bought into the idea that the Lord only responds to certain utterances. Somebody forgot to tell Jesus that.

    Luke 18:10-14, "¹⁰ Two men went up to the temple to pray, one a Pharisee and the other a tax collector. ¹¹ The Pharisee stood and prayed thus with himself, 'God, I thank You that I am not like other men — extortioners, unjust, adulterers, or even as this tax collector.' ¹² 'I fast twice a week; I give tithes of all that I possess.' ¹³ 'And the tax collector, standing afar off, would not so much as raise his eyes to heaven, but beat his breast, saying, 'God, be merciful to me a sinner!' ¹⁴ 'I tell you, this man went down to his house justified rather than the other; for everyone who exalts himself will be humbled and he who humbles himself will be exalted."

    When faith has become sight and our understanding broadened, we will likely be amazed to watch as heaven celebrates that unassuming soul who sat silently on the back pew quietly praying prayers of faith.

2. Down through the decades, it was determined that assembly prayer was just too emotional, and the more educated our leaders became, the more disdainful their attitude toward genuine heartfelt passion before the Lord. Let us quickly agree that emotion for the sake of emotionalism has no place in the local assembly. Let us also quickly agree that there will always be that

segment of the population who has a tendency to be extreme in that respect. Nonetheless, to stifle genuine fervor before the Lord serves to quench the Holy Spirit, robs the wounded soul of open expression, and conveys to us all that honest emotion before the throne of God is completely unacceptable. A sad state of affairs and a pretty accurate description of where we are today in America.

3. What is it that has taken precedence over the assembled prayer meeting? At one time there were almost universal mid-week prayer meetings and they really were prayer meetings. They were not wildly demonstrative prayer meetings, just honest expressions and petitions before the throne of God. Slowly and gradually those changed over to Bible studies and eventually evolved into just another service in an attempt to draw people in. School activities, organized sports, and a thousand other enticing distractions were viewed as more important than being with other believers, exhorting and encouraging. Many of our local churches saw their mid-week service die a slow and painful death, ultimately ceasing to meet completely. In a sincere and well-intended effort pastors and leaders of the local church have searched for some way to draw the people back into the sanctuary. What is the answer? Let us travel back to our Deuteronomy passage:

Deuteronomy 32:16-17, "16They provoked Him to jealousy with foreign gods; With abominations they provoked Him to anger. 17 They sacrificed to demons, not to God, to gods they did not know, to new gods, new arrivals That your fathers did not fear."

The Israelites sacrificed to gods with whom they had no bond, no relationship and by sacrificing to those gods they became adulterers. They were religious for sure, but they chose to set aside the one true God in favor of *"new gods, new arrivals."*

Perhaps that is the best description of our own neglect of assembly prayer. Have we set aside precious communion and communication with our God in favor of offering Him something we created with our own hands, anticipating His blessings because our motivation was good and then marveling that He does not behave as we thought He should? Does that not sound strangely like the lady who cheated at solitaire?

4. In recent months, the Catholic Church has seen momentous happenings. Pope Benedict XVI unexpectedly resigned and the process of appointment of his replacement began. It was a process worthy of attention by the whole population, both Catholic and Protestant because of its historical connotations. In the days following the resignation, however, there was discussion all around concerning whether the Catholic Church would have to modify its stand on significant social issues in order to attract and hold the next generation. Those who subscribe to that belief suppose that the Word can be arbitrarily altered to fit the society in which it lives.

   What has that to do with our assembly prayer stone? Were the leaders of the Catholic Church to take such a monumental step, it would send a message to the masses that God's Word is only vague guidance to be changed and revised at will. At what price would they please the masses? Likewise, it is certainly true that some people will just not come to prayer meetings that might actually come to a regular service. Should we therefore deny the criticality of prayer? Should we just cancel the prayer meeting and try doing everything in our own power? What message does that send to our precious folks? That prayer is negotiable? That prayer is optional? That prayer is not all that important and should be reserved for emergencies? Should pastors and their leadership not set the course and demonstrate the power of faith in prayer before the people they lead?

5. Very few young people under the age of twenty one have ever experienced the uninhibited liberty of open assembly prayer. The perfunctory address is the norm for them. Unfortunately so is mediocrity. So is ritualism. So are empty words and programs. The hands of God are fettered by our prayerlessness because His mighty acts are inexorably tied to our faith-filled prayer.

Do any of these resonate within your heart? I suspect so, even if some of them rile you up a little. Maybe we all need a little riling. There seems to be a disconnect between our understanding of the relationship of assembly prayer to the manifest presence of God in our midst, that which we all crave and pray for in our private prayer times.

If five of us can chase a hundred and a hundred of us can put ten thousand to flight should we not put our shoulders to the same wheel? If God is for us and not against us[68], if it is His good pleasure to give us the kingdom[69], then does it not stand to reason that we should agree together on the issues that matter most?

Not all history speaks of days gone by; we are living right in the midst of it. Are we doomed to live out our era as the Laodicean church, arrogantly believing that we have need of nothing? How will history record this time in the church of America? Will the writers of a future time laud us for our great buildings and timely programs or will they write that we were so consumed with accumulating wealth that we forgot who gives us the power to gain it? Will it read that the church in America could not get it together in the good times, compelling God to turn us over to persecution in order to get our attention?

Absolutely and unequivocally, no! It may take a while to turn this ship around but it is still afloat and we still have divine power at the ready.

The body of Christ in America is conducting itself as a defensive force today, but that was never the design of Christ. We are meant to possess and push back borders, not to passively protect them; we are designed to acquire new territory, not simply hold the line. In the parable of the minas[70] the nobleman told his servants, *"Occupy till I come back."* Occupy. Be strong in the Lord. Possess.

Rise up, pastors! He has heard your petitions before Him, especially those that you pray when it is just you and Him, things you might not pray in open assembly. He has heard and heeded. Pay the price for His sweet presence. Endure the ire of sheep who want their own way. Resist the urge to be like everyone else. Tap into the almighty power of the throne of God. He is waiting for you.

Rise up, leaders! Support your pastor's efforts to return the church to its birthright ….. without grumbling. Will those prayer meetings be a little awkward and stiff? Yes, in the beginning it will be cumbersome, but if you will persist, God will meet you in that place in ways you never imagined.

Rise up, sheep! Lift up your voices before the Lord. Be faithful in your attendance and participation. Return to re-acquaint yourself with the power of assembly prayer. Bring the kids with you. Use those times as spiritual teaching tools. Encourage them to participate.

We stand at a crossroads in the spiritual life of our nation. Will we be remembered as a shining light to future generations here in America and around the world or will we choose to recline in our Laodicean rut? Assemblies across this country are full of strong, born-again, God-loving men and women who are perfectly capable of great exploits through the power of prayer in the ministration of the Holy Spirit. Be like Peter as he threw off his garments and jumped into the water to get to Jesus. I am pretty sure the kids will watch us swim, even if they are just curious to see if we drown on the way!

CHAPTER 7

STONES NUMBER 6 AND 7: COMMITMENT AND CONTINUITY

I know that wisdom can be found in many unexpected settings, but I would have never included the fresh produce department of my local grocery in that list. As I thumped the melons and sniffed pineapples recently, I overheard a conversation between an apparent local resident and a woman whose family had just moved into our small town. The local asked whether it had been a difficult adjustment for the newcomer's family to settle for the limited selection of fresh produce when they had been accustomed to shopping in large, well-stocked supermarkets. Her answer was what took me aback. She replied that it was actually a happy surprise to have fewer choices. She had not realized how many decisions she had had to make every time she went shopping; now there were no decisions. She bought what was available and then invented dishes to use those ingredients to their best advantage. The whole family participated in this new game and actually enjoyed it.

That made me stop to consider just how many decisions we do make in a typical day, choices that many cultures never need deliberate. What time do I need to get up in the morning? What should I have for breakfast? Which glass will I drink from? Do I want to sit at the kitchen table, the breakfast bar, or on the porch? What should I wear to work? Will those shoes go with that outfit? Can I still fit in that outfit? What do the kids need to be ready for their day? Did they have their homework ready? Is it time for the bus? Do they have lunch money? On and on. And that's before breakfast. No kidding. Stop and think about your day. You will be amazed at how many decisions you make in every twenty-four hour period, both large and small. We are a culture of choices and we treasure our right to make these choices.

Our society fell headlong into the pro-choice attitude long before the term came to be the official designator of those who support and promote the right of women to abortions, but the propensity of mankind toward self-will should not come as a surprise:

> *Isaiah 14:12-14, "[12]How art thou fallen from heaven, O Lucifer, son of the morning! how art thou cut down to the ground, which didst weaken the nations! [13]For thou hast said in thine heart, I will ascend into heaven, I will exalt my throne above the stars of God: I will sit also upon the mount of the congregation, in the sides of the north: [14] I will ascend above the heights of the clouds; I will be like the most High."*

Our aspirations may not be as lofty as those of Lucifer, but any choice which draws us away from the cross will ultimately exalt itself against the throne of God.

I once heard it said that any practice which survives within a culture for twenty years will ultimately find a place of acceptance inside the local church; our two stones of commitment and continuity stand witness to that theory. The ever-present (and guardedly treasured) American attitude of self-determination hovers menacingly over our pews and it is that very mindset which has nearly eradicated these two foundational stones. It was not a conscious decision. There was no certain generation which rose up and decided to demand its way in the church. However, we can certainly trace its emergence to the years following and since the social upheaval of the 1960's and the accompanying defiance of authority. No, we cannot set this at the foot of any particular segment of population, nor should we try. We are, instead, like the people surrounding Elijah's altar: ours too was the result of ongoing neglect and decay. It was gradual, almost imperceptible, but glaringly apparent in hindsight. It was my fault and it was your fault and we would do well to steer clear of the tendency to look for someone else to blame.

This might be a good place to re-focus on our two initial questions:

> IS THE CHURCH IN AMERICA LARGELY INEFFECTIVE TODAY BECAUSE OF THE DEPRAVED STATE OF OUR SOCIETY?
>
> OR IS OUR SOCIETY IN THAT CORRUPT STATE BECAUSE THE CHURCH IS LARGELY INEFFECTIVE?

An examination of these two altar stones will help us better understand our quandary, but there must first be agreement that commitment and continuity are both vertical and horizontal.

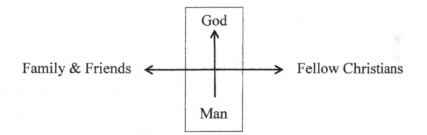

Our foremost commitment is to Christ. That commitment, properly executed, will inevitably lead to continuity, thus the interdependence of these two stones.

Commitment may be costly.

To be clear, let's draw upon secular definitions. We will begin with commitment which is widely defined as the act of pledging or engaging oneself; an obligation or promise that restricts one's freedom of action.

Uh-oh, already we have a problem. We might almost be persuaded to buy into pledging or engaging ourselves within the church today because we no longer place any value on pledging or engaging anyway. On a whim we walk away because it is our choice to make after all. See the problem? And in our eyes, restricting one's freedom of action is always a bad thing.

Paul – as always bold and direct – wrote these words:

> *Colossians 1:19-23, "[19] For it pleased the Father that in Him all the fullness should dwell, [20] and by Him to reconcile all things to Himself, by Him, whether things on earth or things in heaven, having made peace through the blood of His cross. [21] And you, who once were alienated and enemies in your mind by wicked works, yet now He has reconciled [22] in the body of His flesh through death, to present you holy, and blameless, and above reproach in His sight – [23] if indeed you continue in the faith, grounded and steadfast, and are not moved away from the hope of the gospel which you heard, which was preached to every creature under heaven, of which I, Paul, became a minister."*

We who were once alienated by sin have been reconciled to God, He having made peace through the blood of His cross. We who were once alienated by sin can now be presented before God holy, blameless, and above reproach by grace through faith. Having been thus reconciled, it is incumbent upon us to continue in the faith, grounded and steadfast, a theme consistently presented in the Gospels and the Epistles.

Bear in mind that the man who penned these words by the inspiration of the Holy Spirit suffered a little for his faith.

2nd Corinthians 11:23-30, "23 Are they ministers of Christ? (I speak as a fool) I am more; in labours more abundant, in stripes above measure, in prisons more frequent, in deaths oft. 24 Of the Jews five times received I forty stripes save one. 25 Thrice was I beaten with rods, once was I stoned, thrice I suffered shipwreck, a night and a day I have been in the deep; 26 In journeyings often, in perils of waters, in perils of robbers, in perils by mine own countrymen, in perils by the heathen, in perils in the city, in perils in the wilderness, in perils in the sea, in perils among false brethren; 27 In weariness and painfulness, in watchings often, in hunger and thirst, in fastings often, in cold and nakedness. 28 Beside those things that are without, that which cometh upon me daily, the care of all the churches. 29 Who is weak, and I am not weak? who is offended, and I burn not? 30 If I must needs glory, I will glory of the things which concern mine infirmities."

This is like a foreign language to the ear of the American Christian. Teachings of suffering for one's faith have been assailed, criticized, and ridiculed to the point that they have nearly dropped off the radar completely. Syndicated columnist Terry Mattingly recently wrote an article entitled, "Face to Face with 'Nones'." You will remember the 'Nones' from an earlier stone, I am sure. His musings were drawn from a visit to the blog http://marc5solas.com in which the writer shares his views on life in general: "Young people are also supposed to be winners all the time and there's little room for depression or struggle or doubt in many big churches. It's hard to talk about sin, repentance, grace, and forgiveness in that kind of happy talk environment. The church," the writer said, "is simply a place to learn life application principles to achieve a better life. You don't need a crucified Jesus for that."[71]

When was the last time you took stripes on your back or had your life threatened to the point of peril? When was your last shipwreck or stoning? We are quick to defend our American liberty to exercise our faith and I will be at the head of the line to do so, but our examination must be frank and bold. If we openly preached the gospel in America as Apostle Paul did in his day, would we be allowed or would we be imprisoned? How long do you think our society would tolerate Christians who refused to lower their voice when they spoke the name of Jesus? Not long, I dare say.

So what happens to our children or our grandchildren when, God forbid, that liberty, already eroded, disappears completely? How can they possibly reconcile a positive confession gospel with suffering or death? How can the pragmatic teachings of today's leaders prepare future generations for true persecution? What will sustain them when the watered-down, entertainment-driven message fails? I trust that day will never, ever come and that my descendants will worship in a free society even greater than our own, but somebody had better be teaching those precious young people that sometimes there is a price to pay, not to become a Christian for that ransom has already been paid, but for simply being a Christian. In other words, commitment to the gospel can be costly.

We have spoken of commitment to the person of Christ and to the gospel entrusted to us. What about commitment to the members of the body of Christ on earth? What does the Bible teach us about commitment to one another?

The greatest of these is love.

We live in a very mobile world with the average American re-locating every five years so it would be unrealistic to expect the kind of familial ties among Christians enjoyed by generations past, but commitment, allegiance, and loyalty are traits dictated by the Word and are applicable to the church worldwide, generation after generation.

> John 13:35, "*35By this shall all men know that ye are my disciples, if ye have love one to another.*"

Of all the rites and rituals which we might regard as typifying Christianity, the Bible sets the bar on one: love for one another. In the early church the Christians were renowned for their love for one another, bringing forth such exclamations as, "See how these Christians love one another." (Tertullian) We will not be comprehended as disciples of Christ by the number of services we attend or the way we dress or by how many Bible passages we memorize. Life practices such as study and prayer, though admirable, do not distinguish us as His disciples.

On different occasions down through the years, the Lord has allowed me to visit in low-income, high-crime neighborhoods. It occurred to me one evening that it would be ever so much easier if I were a nun clothed in an easily recognizable habit. If one of those dear sisters walked down the street people immediately understood her motive was pure. She could establish a rapport in five minutes that would take me months or even years to cultivate. Such is the case with love. It is not about external accoutrements; it is not something you can put on and take off at will; neither is it evidenced by how much you know about the Bible. The world is not looking for rite or ritual. They are searching for something that eludes them: real love.

1st John 1:6 charges all Christians of all times of all places to walk just as He walked, and that translates to loving horizontal commitment. You may be one of those whose employment or family structure requires periodic re-location but wherever you are, be committed to love. Maintain former relationships when you move; cultivate commitment in your new location, be known for your quiet steadfastness and faithfulness. Let your reputation be one of compassion and tenderness toward fellow Christians, both here and abroad. Be proactive in your love.

An interconnected whole

Love of this magnitude does not just happen; it is cultivated and nurtured which very naturally leads us into our second stone: continuity, defined as a continuous or connected whole.

Several years ago we were invited to a nearby city to dine with my sister and her family. After going through the usual rigmarole of eatery choices, we settled on a somewhat dumpy little place on a tree-lined side street which catered mostly to university students. The owners had selected a truly nifty name for their restaurant, one which would have told a reasonable person to dine elsewhere. We did not go elsewhere; we walked right in and imagine our surprise when it was exactly as advertised in the name. Go figure.

Can we take that little café experience over into the local church? Our namesake flies a universal banner of love, joy, peace, longsuffering, kindness, goodness, faithfulness, gentleness, and self-control.[72] People who walk through our café door have the right to expect that our name matches the reality of what they will experience within, the demonstrative love that will tell the world that we are His disciples.

I find myself mourning the death of the elderly in a new way recently. The generation that is passing away right now (in 2013) is the last who can remember firsthand the old days of real commitment and continuity. Their passing leaves our society with a sense of having lost our bearings, bringing an indefinable sense of vulnerability. These folks were no different than you or I, no better, no worse; they were no more spiritual than we are. Perhaps the strength and steadfastness they represent came as a result of the hardships of the times they endured. Their legacy of commitment, both to God and to mankind, and the follow-on continuity gave us all a little better understanding of our identity and an appreciation of this truth: we cannot fully comprehend who we are unless we know where we came from.

How do we cultivate these traits? Teach Jesus. Teach Him prophesied. Teach Him born of a virgin. Teach Him living a perfect, sinless life. Teach Him powerful. Teach Him humble. Teach Him crucified. Teach Him resurrected. Teach Him glorified. Teach Him at the right hand of the Father. Teach Him coming back. Teach Him comforting. Teach Him defending. Teach Him ever present. Teach Jesus. Teach Him softly. Teach Him boldly. Teach Him unconditionally loving.

That is how our kids and our grandkids and generations to come will grasp who they are and where they came from. They did not come from Boston or Seattle. Their roots are not in Scotland or New Zealand. Their heritage is not earthly. Those beginnings are disposable; they will pass away. Teach them that they were prophesied. Teach them that they can have a new birth. Teach them that His grace is sufficient for their need, no matter how black and sordid. Teach them that the power of the very throne of God is theirs for the asking. Teach them that humility is not weakness, but power. Teach them of the bloody cross and teach them to take up their own cross. Teach them that because He lives, they never have to fear death. Teach them that they are "*heirs; heirs of God, and joint heirs with Christ; if so be that we suffer with him, that we may be also glorified together.*"[73] Teach them that He "*ever liveth to make intercession for them*" and that they are never left alone to their own devices.[74] Teach them that the world system has been telling them lies of destruction; tell them that Jesus is coming back for His own. Teach them that even when mother and father and friends have turned their backs and walked away, Jesus will never leave them nor forsake them. Teach them that Jesus is the defender of the helpless. Teach them that He speaks so softly that a feather could ride delicately upon His voice and yet mountains melt like wax at His presence. Teach them about grace.

Teach Jesus.

CHAPTER 8

STONE NUMBER 8: MUTUAL RESPECT

Our first five stones (reverential fear, salvation, the Word, consecration, and prayer) are foundational to the stability and steadfastness of our walk as disciples of Jesus. The remaining stones are just natural offshoots of the first five. The final seven stones will fall naturally into place when the first five have been properly established and perpetuated; conversely, when attention to the first five fails then the final seven cannot long survive. Our most recent two stones, commitment and continuity, are simply extensions of the first five, and that is precisely what we will see in our examination of the state of mutual respect within the body of Christ.

The Israelites who gathered around Elijah on Mount Carmel represented an all-inclusive assembly. The men, women, and children of Israel had crawled out of bed that morning, thinking to be about life as usual. Dinner was planned, errands were charted for the day, and the kids did what kids do. Little did they know that they were about to be summoned to participate in what would become a Super Bowl size, eternally renowned event. Some of those folks were wealthier than others; some were younger than others; some were better educated than others; some were leaders and some were everyday citizens, but on that particular day they all stood on the same turf, a portrait of equality because God is no respecter of persons.[75]

Likewise, the church is made up of the entire spectrum of humanity and in that context every man, woman, boy, and girl occupies equal standing and is deserving of respect and high regard, but once again our secular culture has seeped menacingly into the church and in our weakened state we have either failed to discern it or we lack the will to fight back.

The commonality of you and me

Despite our differences, we have a lot in common, you and me and all humanity. We share the unavoidable demand for sustenance and protection from the elements, we share the need for covering for our physical body, and we share the more intangible needs of the mind and the emotions. There are some very basic emotional and psychological needs which apply to every single person walking this earth, whether on the urban streets, through the rows of corn, or in uncharted regions. They are not unique to any particular culture or societal element; they ignore social strata and religious affiliations. Helen Saul in her treatise on phobias wrote, "The first step – understanding your emotions – is to learn about your psychological needs. Examples of needs that are frequently described include:

1. The need to give and receive love

2. The need to belong and feel secure

3. The need to explore and learn

4. The need to create

5. The need for relationships

6. The need to find purpose and meaning in life."[76]

A nurturing environment in which people are able to realize these benefits must above all be one of mutual respect. Jesus so meticulously acknowledged all of these that it would seem a foregone conclusion that they would be evident to overflowing within His own body, the church, but they are not. They are, in fact, conspicuously absent.

Galatians 6:7, "⁷ Do not be deceived, God is not mocked;
for whatever a man sows, that he will also reap."

Sow sparingly, reap sparingly. Sow abundantly, reap abundantly. So much emphasis has been placed on the financial ramifications of this teaching (which indeed do apply) that an entire sphere of relational sowing has been sorely neglected. If I expect to be respected, then I need to disburse respect. If I expect to be provoked within the body to explore and learn, then it is incumbent upon me to provoke others likewise. If I am searching for purpose and meaning in life, then I must extend myself in encouragement and stimulate the creativity of others, but do you know what has happened in that realm? We have subscribed to words like "*karma*" taken straight from the lexicon of idolatry rooted in Hinduism and Buddhism. Do good and good will follow; do bad and look out. Is that not just another way of saying sowing and reaping? What could that possibly hurt? It is just a little word. First and foremost, by virtue of such thinking we have given space to idolatry within the church, and for that we need to repent, pure and simple. Secondly, subscribing to such thinking assigns what should be the comfort of precious interrelationships to some vaporous force of the universe rather than subjecting each one to the very pervasive oversight of the Word of God and the very personage of Christ. The end result? The sense – either consciously or otherwise – that there is another go-round to this life, negating personal responsibility toward other human beings. It's all about me.

There is one Truth and that is the Word of God. You cannot bring in one smidgen of idolatry and bring it to bear on Godly principles. It is God who gives when we sow, not some negligible universal fog of the lie of enlightenment. To assign the benefits of the Word to anything other than God Himself is idolatrous.

The uncommon one anothers

We could go into a lengthy study of the "one another" passages of Jesus' words and they would tell us all we need know about mutual respect, but most of you already know them anyway so instead we will look at only one Scripture to address each of the emotional and psychological needs listed above:

1. The need to give and receive love

    1ˢᵗ Thessalonians 4:9, "⁹But concerning brotherly love you have no need that I should write to you, for you yourselves are taught by God to love one another."

2. The need to belong and feel secure

    Mark 9:50, "⁵⁰ Salt is good (beneficial); but if salt has lost its saltness, how will you restore {the saltness to} it? Have salt within yourselves and be at peace and live in harmony with one another." Amplified Bible

3. The need to explore and learn

    2ⁿᵈ Timothy 2:15, "¹⁵ Be diligent to present yourself approved to God, a worker who does not need to be ashamed, rightly dividing the word of truth."

4. The need to create

    Genesis 1:26-27, "²⁶Then God said, 'Let Us make man in Our image, according to Our likeness; let them have dominion over the fish of the sea, over the birds of the air, and over the cattle, over all the earth, and over every creeping thing that creeps on the earth.'

²⁷So God created man in His own image; in the image of God He created him; male and female He created them."

5. The need for relationships

    2ⁿᵈ Corinthians 13:11-14, "¹¹Finally, brethren, farewell. Become complete. Be of good comfort, be of one mind, live in peace; and the God of love and peace will be with you. ¹²Greet one another with a holy kiss. ¹³All the saints greet you. ¹⁴ The grace of the Lord Jesus Christ, and the love of God, and the communion of the Holy Spirit be with you all. Amen."

6. The need to find purpose and meaning in life

    Jeremiah 29:11, "¹¹For I know the thoughts that I think toward you, says the Lord, thoughts of peace and not of evil, to give you a future and a hope."

Again with the sheep

One of the first lessons that I had to learn as a minister of the gospel was the value of each and every sheep, a lesson that did not come easy. For the sake of my own convenience I put off helping a lost friend find some of the emotional comforts we just studied. Her decades long marriage had just ended abruptly and her life had quite literally fallen apart. "Call me sometime and we will sit down over a cup of coffee and talk," I said, thinking to lead her to the Lord. Within a few days she committed suicide. Did she need someone to speak words of love and assurance to her? Without a doubt, yes. Would it have made a difference if she had? Only God knows. I resigned the call to minister about thirty five times that day but the Lord kept rejecting my resignation. What He did teach me through this experience was this: Jesus died for that person; He loved that lady, once so full of life. How dare I neglect loving respect?

At the risk of offending your sensibilities, let me share a thought with you. I recently visited the children's section of a major bookstore for the sole purpose of ferreting out the subject of mutual respect from a child's point of view. I have found that some of the most profound statements on any given topic can be found there in the little twelve page books. I examined several but nothing that really spoke to me. Finally I asked one of their knowledgeable clerks if she had any suggestions. "How old is the child?" she asked. I paused for a moment before confessing that it was not for a child but for adults. She could not suppress a little chuckle but allowed as how she probably did not have anything which would be helpful, and I turned to go my way but then my eye fell on an intriguing cover carrying the title, "Everybody Poops."[77] Let me tell you, folks, it is the truth. Sheep leave sheep droppings all over the place and not everyone you extend yourself toward is going to receive your acts of respect with open arms. In fact, some are likely to throw it to the floor and stomp on it, but that is not the point. The point is that Jesus died for that person and He wants to bless that person; your part is to return relational respect to the local church and allow Him to take care of the rest.

To our wonderful spiritual leaders across this nation, do not presume that your people know that you respect them. Show them by your actions; loose them in their giftings to bless the body of Christ. They are not assets; they are fully equipped children of God. Shape them. Respect them. Loose them. Yes, even the kids.

CHAPTER 9

STONE NUMBER 9: MARRIAGE AND THE FAMILY

Dearly beloved.

Are there any other words in the English language which so easily provoke fairytale like responses? Immediately we seem to find ourselves immersed in an atmosphere of grace and beauty rarely found elsewhere in our society. The words evoke visions of romance, endless possibilities, and storybook endings. Surrounded by such romance, jeans-clad girls are beautifully transformed into gowned ladies, somehow more poised and confident than usual. They seem to float down the aisle. Men magically morph into Cary Grants or Sean Connerys, strong and stately in their tuxedos. Life looks good when we hear "dearly beloved."

Ephesians 5:25, "²⁵Husbands, love your wives, just as Christ also loved the church and gave Himself for her,"

The Bible has much to say about the husband and wife relationship, but it is this one command which allows for the dearly beloved dream to last a lifetime. Inside the framework of the love of Christ, all things are possible.....even in America.

I once asked my own grandchildren in what period of time they would have liked to live. Most of them responded almost immediately by identifying positively with the television show "Happy Days." With that remarkable response, I broadened the survey to a fairly small but representative general audience, and lo and behold, the answer was the same, and the response was inevitably followed by what it was that so connected them to the Cunninghams:

1. The father always came home at the end of the day and spent time with the family. He interacted with the kids when they had problems or challenges or needed encouragement.

2. The father was *their* father.

3. The mother was always there and she was always available. She was happy and proud to be a stay at home mom and was completely devoted to the father and the family.

4. The mother was *their* mother.

5. Friends stayed friends.

6. Families stayed together.

This would be a good place to launch into a glut of statistical data to back up the theory that marriage and family are in jeopardy in America, but I doubt that is necessary. We are in deep trouble, folks; you know it and I know it. Nor do we need to catalog the various maladies that assault the home. Read the newspaper. Watch the news. Listen to the conversation in the supermarket aisles. We know our families are on the precipice of destruction, held back only by the grace of God.

Of all the final seven stones, this particular one may be the most crucial since every aspect of a healthy society rests upon order in the home so it begs a slight variation on our original question:

Is the state of marriage and the home in America self-destructing because of the depraved state of our society?

Or are our marriages and homes in that deteriorated state because the Church has become ineffective in its teaching?

Remember our earlier assertion: it is not the world's fault that we are in a mess. The world will do what the world will do. It is our place as disciples of Jesus to set the standard for righteous marriages and blessed homes, and since the Bible is the only absolute truth in existence, then it follows that it is our only source for action. Tragically, somewhere along the line we dropped the ball, assigning such instruction to television, and then movies, and then the internet. Generation by generation we increasingly abdicated our God-given charge to train up our children, relinquishing our most precious national treasure to the dictates of a lost and savage world. Is it any wonder then that our kids accept unrestrained sex as the equivalent of love? Are we really surprised at their skewed comprehension of marriage when their only point of reference grows out of a one-hour weekly television show in which men and women frolic suggestively with the opposite sex, competing to win the prize of marriage? The women are perfectly made up, covering every flaw and blemish, and so that must be the way a wife should always look, right? Their clothing, designed by notable designers, is seductive, enticing and beguiling. Their surroundings are opulent, and their sole calling is to figure out ways to manipulate their way to victory…. marriage. There is no limit to what these women will do to win the prize, no limit. I do believe that even Jezebel might blush at some of their enticements. It is no better when the tables are turned and the guys are on display. These men are unbelievably patient and understanding…. like all husbands. They never sweat or have bad breath and are remarkably conscientious about picking up their socks and underwear. They are virtual Prince

Charmings, wooing and courting and so willing....even anxious.... to hear all about her feelings. You and I might choose to watch such nonsense and walk away knowing that everything we just witnessed is a gigantic stack of fertilizer, but our kids do not because nobody has taught them how marriage really should be.

'Til death do ye part

Marriage – one man and one woman – was established as one of the first creative acts of God and so it is no wonder then that the reverberations of marriage are inestimable. As science strives to comprehend creation of the universe, so have psychologists struggled to grasp the extent of the mental, emotional, and physical violence of divorce upon the participants and the children. By the same token, these same folks have yet to fully explore the positive contributions of a good marriage.

I was visited once by a woman who had been repeatedly beaten and battered by the events of life. She entered with the "life is good" smiling face we all wear occasionally, but as her story unfolded I heard heartbreak after heartbreak, built upon heartbreak, followed by heartbreak. Her broken condition had led to all sorts of strongholds, most of which seemed to be directly traceable to her early childhood and her own parents' marriage. She sat subdued in the chair having nothing left to offer me. She had no tears left. I asked about her parents and her early upbringing and was somewhat surprised when she sat straight up in the chair, smiled, and assured me that her childhood had been very normal. Good Mom. Good Dad. Pretty routine stuff, she assured me. We talked about other things in life for a while and as we spoke I learned that her father's presence was intermittent at best. He managed to live at home once in a while but mostly he was away "visiting friends." The mother would wait on the father, knowing full well that his friends were other women who were enjoying the company of her husband, and she grew progressively more and more angry, eventually turning to drugs and alcohol for comfort. That was the incubation environment for the broken woman before me. She saw it as normal because that was all she knew. Thank God for grace; thank God that He takes broken lives and makes them new.

On rare occasions we are fortunate enough to cross paths with someone who forever changes our lives. Such was my privilege when I first met my mentor and friend, Becky Ryan, who along with her husband, Dr. John Edw. Ryan, pastored in ways almost unheard of in today's religious world. He and his family forfeited the luxuries and comforts of American society, choosing instead to live dependent upon the Lord. Though an articulate, highly educated and intellectual man, he chose to work with the outcasts of society accepting into their loving care children who had been labeled disposable by their biological parents. My friend and I visited them one day, a simple errand to drop off some clothing for the kids. We fully intended to drop off the clothing and be on our merry way, but they would have none of that; instead, they whisked us away on a tour of the facility where they introduced us to the children, toured the housing facility and especially the kitchen where they fed lots of hungry mouths, and finally we visited the print shop where Dr. Ryan trained the young men in a practical trade. As we stood curbside saying our goodbyes a car with out of state plates pulled up, the window on the passenger side was lowered, and a baby was thrust through the window and deposited in the waiting arms of the Ryans, another casualty of marriage gone awry. That visit dates back some thirty-five years but this heartrending scene is as fresh in my mind as it was that cold day on the sidewalk. It was a scene to be repeated again and again at that little refuge as parents sought to find a way out of the very difficult task of parenting. To their credit, they did assure the children were in a place where they would be cared for and loved.

A true follower of Christ should be shocked by such actions. How could any parent simply drop their child off curbside and drive away, leaving the baby at the mercy of strangers? While we may not be guilty of physically depositing our children curbside, might we not be found guilty as a society of relegating the spiritual training of our children to the world? Babysitters and day care facilities - even the really great ones – are no substitute for the loving and nurturing arms of Mom and Dad. Most of the time these folks spend more hours per day with our children than we do and so early instruction, for good or otherwise, comes in our absence.

As we load our children on buses each morning or drop them off at the school, are we fully aware of what they will be taught that day? Do we really comprehend all that they are going to face? Home school is not always a valid option, private schools may be financially out of reach, but an attuned parent backed up by a Bible-teaching local church can fend off the destructive intent of the enemy and teach life-giving truths.

The sky is right where God put it.

I determined early on to approach this stone from an upbeat, proactive point of view, resisting the urge to do my Henny Penny imitation. Indeed the sky does seem to be falling in many ways, but we are not without remedy.

> *Psalms 46:1-2,7, "¹God is our refuge and strength, a very present help in trouble. ²Therefore will not we fear, even though the earth be removed, and though the mountains be carried into the midst of the sea; .... ⁷ The Lord of hosts is with us; The God of Jacob is our refuge."*

Our hearts are still beating, we have air in our lungs, and God is still on the throne! It is never too late, but the church must take steps now to stop the tsunami of destruction. Teach, teach, teach. Healthy marriages are not second nature to mankind; it must be taught. Right standing among husband, wife, and child goes against our fleshly nature; it must be taught. In the flesh, children want to rebel; wives want to rule; and husbands want to relegate their responsibility to someone else. The world affirms those tendencies, calls them good. Television almost invariably portrays the man of the house as an inept, bumbling weakling while children are portrayed as rulers. Our kids see those images from the time they are born. Why should we gasp with surprise when that is the way they grow up to behave?

How can we possibly hope to bequeath relational stability when we ourselves stand on shifting sand? We immerse ourselves in the only infallible user's manual, the only source of absolute truth, the Bible. God created a helper comparable to man[78], someone who would help and aid him, not only for the man, Adam, but for all his male descendants in generations to come. The helper would complement Adam's life and provide companionship on a very personal level. That was the relationship created by God in Eden, a perfect environment. Adam was real glad and called her "*Ishshah*" or woman[79].

Life was pretty good in the garden and we have no inkling that Adam and Eve were anything but wonderfully content until that fateful day when the woman went shopping for fruit. We know the woeful story so we will cut right to the scene of the curse found in Genesis 3:14-16. Now everything had changed. Now the woman was going to have the privilege of frequent vomiting, living in doctors' offices, swelling to blimp proportions for nine months, and then celebrate by hours of serious bodily suffering surrounded by people who want to assure her it is not all that bad. I have three children of my own. Trust me, honey, it is bad. Worth it, mind you, but it is no walk in the park. And if that was not bad enough, by her very own nature under the curse, her desire would be toward her husband and….wait for it, wait for it….he would rule over her. Oh, Grandma Eve, whatever did you do!?!

Wipe that smile off, guys; you did not fare any better. You remember that job you were thrilled to get but quickly grew tired of? In the curse. The fatigue you face at the end of the day? In the curse. The two steps forward and three steps back dance that life seems to hand you? That would be the curse. And that beautiful woman who creates your honey-do list every weekend? Well, that is just her desiring you and your headship. Blasted curse!

Our original grandfather and grandmother did not let the grass grow under their feet long (probably because they had no idea what it all meant at that point), and soon they were cranking out offspring, and those babies entered the world not in the perfect environment of times past, but under the curse, in need of reconciliation and divine redemption. Those boys had no school system to blame so we cannot blame the teachers or the curriculum. They did not have a lazy, good-for-nothing father; to the contrary it would seem that Adam was quite industrious. Their mother did not work outside the home, although I think we can safely assume that Eve worked plenty hard inside the home. Their food did not contain contaminants so we cannot blame pollutants. No movies. No television. No internet. The point at hand is this: Cain and Abel spawned descendants whose marriages were forged, not in the original paradise, but in a fallen world. They made their choices in that environment and they did not fare well. The Bible gives us ubiquitous examples of infidelities, bigamy, polygamy, concubines, prostitutes, and an endless list of sexual perversions. Solomon was spot on when he wrote:

> *Ecclesiastes 1:9-10, "⁹That which has been is what will be, That which is done is what will be done, And there is nothing new under the sun. ¹⁰Is there anything of which it may be said, 'See, this is new?' It has already been in ancient times before us."*

In spite of our immorality and corruption, we have found nothing new. Sin was sin then and sin is sin now.

Not surprisingly, God's design for marriage was assaulted with a vengeance from the get-go for out of that created union springs a myriad of life-sustaining merits, to name only a few: healthy interpersonal relationships, life skills, physical health, stability, security, a strong self-image, contentment, and the assurance that at the end of the day there will be acceptance and a sense of belonging, knowing that your spouse is unconditionally on your side and has your best interest at heart. Sounds heavenly, doesn't it? Unfortunately, the opposite is also true when the family unit crumbles.

The words of the New Testament confirm God's design for husband and wife relationship. One of the most complete passages of instruction can be found here:

> Ephesians 5:22-33, "*²²Wives, submit yourselves unto your own husbands, as unto the Lord. ²³ For the husband is the head of the wife, even as Christ is the head of the church: and he is the saviour of the body. ²⁴Therefore as the church is subject unto Christ, so let the wives be to their own husbands in every thing. ²⁵Husbands, love your wives, even as Christ also loved the church, and gave himself for it; ²⁶That he might sanctify and cleanse it with the washing of water by the word, ²⁷That he might present it to himself a glorious church, not having spot, or wrinkle, or any such thing; but that it should be holy and without blemish. ²⁸So ought men to love their wives as their own bodies. He that loveth his wife loveth himself. ²⁹For no man ever yet hated his own flesh; but nourisheth and cherisheth it, even as the Lord the church: ³⁰For we are members of his body, of his flesh, and of his bones. ³¹For this cause shall a man leave his father and mother, and shall be joined unto his wife, and they two shall be one flesh. ³²This is a great mystery: but I speak concerning Christ and the church. ³³Nevertheless let every one of you in particular so love his wife even as himself; and the wife see that she reverence her husband.*"

Most women stopped reading after the first three words. Even Christian women who truly love their husbands sometimes find this section of Scripture pretty repugnant. Yea, even I have had some heartburn over this one in times gone by. I find it especially amusing when men who are lost as gooses and have absolutely no knowledge of the Word of God quote this passage in order to win an argument with their wives.

If this passage was worded a little differently (and I am not purporting that it should be) men would find it just as unsavory because their charge as husbands is ever so much more demanding than simple oversight. He is charged with loving his wife as *"Christ also loved the Church and gave Himself for it."* As a woman, I could come much closer to fulfilling the submit command than any man could ever come to loving as Christ loved.

Placing the stone

From the Garden to America, marriage has been under relentless assault and it continues be so today, so how does this stone get back in place? How can we possibly hope to turn the tide? Tis a daunting charge for sure. We did not get in this mess in one generation and we are not going to get out of it in one generation; we must be content to play our part by teaching our children so that they will then be equipped to teach theirs and so on. In order for that to happen, teachings on marriage *must be restored into the everyday life of the church.*

If your local assembly has a nursery, then train up workers who will pray over those little ones, people who will speak life and health into the future marriages and families of those precious babies. I simply cannot overemphasize this next point: You do not know what those kids go home to after services. You may think you do, but you do not. Compared to our wonderful children's teachers, I have had relatively little time working with children in ministry and yet I have encountered three separate incidents of children who found ways to tell me and the other leaders that they were suffering unspeakable horrors at home. Does prayer work? Does God answer prayer or not? Does God watch over those trusting, helpless beings? Will He not move for them?

> *Matthew 19:13-15, "¹³Then were there brought unto him little children, that he should put his hands on them, and pray: and the disciples rebuked them. ¹⁴But Jesus said,*

*Suffer little children, and forbid them not, to come unto
me: for of such is the kingdom of heaven. [15]And he laid his
hands on them, and departed thence."*

Of such is the kingdom of heaven. Tell those little people stories of
growing up and meeting the one who God has designed for them. Make
it fun. Tell them often. Pray lovingly.

Teach the young people about proper dating practices. Talk openly
about self-respect and self-control and the high value one should place
on intimacy and its proper time. Set in place the comprehension of
marriage as a lifetime walk.

Time travel

Bear with me for a moment while I quote for you from The Gospel
Primer, a textbook published in 1899 and used by teachers in elementary
settings of the day. The object of the lesson is at least two-pronged: to
develop reading skills and simultaneously portray an image of what a
normal home…..a godly home… looks like.

The first is entitled, "Mother Love."
Mother. The mother. The good mother. The good
mother loves God, and God loves her.
Child. The child. The good child. The child is good.
The good child loves his mother. My mother is good to
me. I am my mother's child. Do I love my mother? If I
love her, I will be good to her.

The next is entitled, "Brother Love."
Brother. My brother. My good brother. My brother
loves me. He is good to me.
Sister. **Dear**. My sister. My dear sister. She is good to
me. My sister loves her mother and her brother. My

sister is my mother's child, and so is my brother. Our mother loves all her children, and we love her. All good children love their mother.

The next one is entitled, "Father Love."

Father. Our dear father. Our father is a good man. He loves my mother, and she loves him. Our father loves his children, and they all love him. He is a good father to us, and we will all be good children. God loves my father and my mother. He loves my brother and my sister. He loves me. If I love God, I will love my brothers and sisters.

The final one talks about "The Happy Home":

Happy. My father and mother are God's children. They love him, and he loves them.

Home. Our home is a happy home. Our father and mother love their children, and love each other. Their children love them, and love one another.

Makes. Love makes us happy. We love God and one another; so he puts his love upon us. No home can be happy without love. In heaven all is love. If it were not so, heaven would not be a happy place.

Is that not a little too elementary, you say? Not in a world where certainty is a rare commodity. Our children are surrounded by chaos and confusion. What was good is now bad and what was once viewed as appalling is now viewed as normal. Up is now down. Black and white are obsolete and gray rules in their place.

Three friends and I visited a hospital several years ago to check on a surgery patient. Ever since I turned fifty I seem to be unable to pass up any bathroom facility and so I excused myself to the ladies room while the three of them waited outside. The restroom was empty except for me and a woman who was standing in front of the mirror touching up her makeup. When I came out of the restroom there were my three friends lined up against the wall, speechless and since that did not happen with those three very often I knew something was up. One of them finally regained his voice enough to ask if I had noticed the person who had just come out the door. It turns out the make-up artist was not a woman at all, but a man in drag. That was some fifteen years ago. Can you imagine who is next to your son or your daughter in public restrooms? Can you even conceive the pressure they are under? Are we equipping them to face such madness? Absolutely not.

I know it is a little difficult to imagine today's child giving voice to such elementary, unambiguous reading material (nor do I advocate a return to the 1899 Primer), but in a world filled with uncertainty our children need clear, concise direction. They desperately need someone to plant basic Biblical instruction in their hearts, leaving little wiggle room for interpretation. Inculcate. Say it this way; say it that way. Sing it. Teach it. Be innovative. Be creative. Teach them on paper, computers, iPods, and tablets. Let the Holy Spirit inspire you to find ways to plant seeds of truth with effectiveness. Pray with them. Pray with clarity. Encourage the kids to pray over their own futures. Encourage them to pray specifically.

What about adults? Is it too late for someone who has grown to adulthood under the world system to change all that they believe concerning marriage even if they were not taught as a child, even if they have already offended God's design? Aren't you glad that we serve a God with Whom it is never, ever too late so long as we are seeking Him with a repentant heart? Indeed, we should all shout "YES" because, "*as it is written, There is none righteous, no, not one:*"[80]

I myself have been the bloody target of many Christians because of my own divorce some forty-seven years ago, condemned to burn in hell by their measure. I thank God for the young Baptist minister and his wife who ministered the word of love to me back then. Even then it took me years to forgive myself and during that time I sat in pews and sung the songs of praise with a smile on my lips and a heart that broke with every word and wounds of self-condemnation which could not heal. Freedom did not come for me until the truth of the Word of God compelled me into the fold of His grace. Having now ministered for over twenty years I can say with confidence that every congregation has its share of bludgeoned Christians who are searching for the unmitigated truth of the word of grace. They are there among you every Sunday. Pastors and teachers, I encourage you to preach and to teach the unblemished truth before the people. The Holy Spirit will take that truth and minister grace to the individual need. If reconciliation, reconciliation. If repentance, repentance. If forgiveness, forgiveness. If hope, hope. If new dreams where old ones died a violent death, then dreams.

This stone perhaps more than any other will require dogged determination on the part of church leadership. It will not be accomplished in one sermon or one four-week series per year; it does not have a completion day. It will take decades and more decades. It must permeate every aspect of church life. Encourage families to worship as one on Sunday. Promote the family at fellowship events, being careful to remain ultra-sensitive to one-parent families, single folks, children without parents present, etc. Does one soul have more value than another? Does one family unit demand greater honor than another? God forbid!

Pursue this stone with tenacity. Pray over it. Pray over the families in your own local congregation and ask the Holy Spirit how you might touch each one with healing words and life giving deeds. If you will commit to that, you will begin to witness transformations of Divine proportions. And generations to come.....well they will owe you a debt of gratitude.

CHAPTER 10

STONE NUMBER 10: CONTENTMENT

Be content. Sounds incredibly simple, and yet of all the charges presented to us in the Word of God, simple contentment is far and away one of the toughest to observe. Sadly, it does not even matter what the topic is: a cruise, clothes in our closets, shoes on our feet, cars in the garage, bigger garages, houses, jobs, and, yes, money. We just want more. I cannot imagine any better example than Black Friday, a day on which normally sane men and women transform into ferocious plunderers, willing to trample other human beings in order to possess some trinket.

Why are we that way? Way back in the beginning of days God said, *"Let Us make man in our image, according to Our likeness; let them have dominion ……."*[81] We are created with a God-given drive to possess and occupy and that is one directive we follow with abandon. In the pre-fall environment that manifested as God's created beings administering their charge; in the post-fall environment our fleshly nature cries out for self-indulgent gratification. What started out in Eden as an honorable and worthy charge became distorted and grossly perverted at the time of the fall.

Have you ever known someone who felt compelled to trump everything anyone else said? If you mentioned that you had been to Hawaii, then they had gone twice. If you had skied some noteworthy slope, then they had hit that one running backward with only one ski.

If you had worked really hard and had finally succeeded in saving up enough money to buy a nice used car, they reminisced about the time when they had bought one of those but theirs was new and had leather seats. That kind of thing. Does a name come to mind? I knew one of those people years ago, a man who became a part of our large circle of military friends, some of whom had some pretty sound equestrian skills, and as always, the one friend would scornfully announce that he had ridden on ranches all over the western U. S. Several months later we all decided to go to a local stable and ride together. The stable manager and workers greeted us and talked with each of us to determine our level of riding experience so that they could match us with suitable steeds. There were several of us and it was quite a task for those folks but wouldn't you know that Mr. Seen-It-All-Done-It-All proudly declared that he could ride any horse they had....and so they gave him one of their friskier mounts. (Mine, by the way, was probably a retired plow horse.) We all mounted up and began to amble pleasantly around the grassy pasture, talking and having a big old time when all of a sudden a shadowy blur flew by us all. Whatever it was it was moving fast and screaming loudly. Not only could this guy not sit a horse, but he could not begin to manage the reins, and so it is with us.

Apostle Paul addressed this dilemma here:

> *Philippians 4:11-13, "[11] Not that I speak in regard to need, for I have learned in whatever state I am, to be content. [12] I know how to be abased* (live humbly) *and I know how to abound* (live in prosperity). *Everywhere and in all things I have learned both to be full and to be hungry, both to abound and to suffer need. [13] I can do all things through Christ who strengthens me."*

We love Verse 13; not so much Verses 11 and 12.

Paul was not born with a highly developed sense of contentment; he did not know how to live humbly and how to prosper rightly until he had gone through some of life's challenges. He said *"....I have learned...*" He learned by experiencing both extremes firsthand. He had lived sacrificially for the sake of the gospel and so he knew how to live humbly, and yet there were also times in his life when his needs were met in abundance, and that requires a whole different kind of faith. Paul learned how to manage the reins of his life.

An explanation of two definitions will help us to see ourselves more accurately:

1. Satisfy: To gratify, appease, pacify, please. To satisfy is to meet to the full one's wants, expectations, etc.

2. Content: To have enough to keep one from being disposed to find fault or complain.

I am not certain that it is even possible to satisfy the wants and expectations of most Americans. We are very much like the parable of the rich man who ran out of room to store his plentiful crops, and so he asked himself, *"What shall I do, because I have no room where to bestow my fruits?"*[82] His solution was to tear down the old barns and build bigger and better ones, and then he said, *"I will say to my soul, Soul, thou hast much goods laid up for many years; take thine ease, eat, drink, and be merry."* This was a parable and not a fairy tale with a happily ever after conclusion; that night the man would die, leaving his precious stuff to someone else who had not labored for it at all. The bottom line of the parable goes like this, *"So is he that layeth up treasure for himself, and is not rich toward God."*

There is nothing wrong with working hard and accumulating wealth for wealth, in and of itself, does not offend the Word of God, provided it is acquired honestly and ethically and so long as it does not begin to occupy the throne of our hearts.

"And he said unto them, Take heed, and beware of covetousness: for a man's life consisteth not in the abundance of the things which he possesseth."

Timothy wrote even more clearly when he said:

> *1ˢᵗ Timothy 6:5-10, ", ⁵Perverse disputings of men of corrupt minds, and destitute of the truth, supposing that gain is godliness: from such withdraw thyself. ⁶ But godliness with contentment is great gain. ⁷ For we brought nothing into this world, and it is certain we can carry nothing out. ⁸ And having food and raiment let us be therewith content. ⁹ But they that will be rich fall into temptation and a snare, and into many foolish and hurtful lusts, which drown men in destruction and perdition. ¹⁰ For the love of money is the root of all evil: which while some coveted after, they have erred from the faith, and pierced themselves through with many sorrows."*

Gain is not godliness; gain is not a barometer of how much God loves you. Look around you. This fallen world is full to the brim and running over with gain of every variety, but devoid of true godliness. Any way we look at it, the enemy of contentment is rooted in covetousness which immediately leads our minds back to the Ten Commandments.

> *Exodus 20:17, "¹⁷You shall not covet your neighbor's house; you shall not covet your neighbor's wife, nor his male servant, nor his female servant, nor his ox, nor his donkey, nor anything that is your neighbor's."*

The Ten Commandments may be our word association gut response, but coveting goes way back, all the way to Eden. The word translated *"covet"* in the above verse is the same word used in Genesis Chapter 2 to describe the trees in Eden, that were *"pleasant to the sight"* and it is also the same word used in Genesis Chapter 3 to describe Eve's perception of the forbidden tree as something *"to be desired."* Eve coveted, the man acquiesced, they ate and the rest is history. That forces us to acknowledge covetousness by its true name: sin. There has been a sharp decline in the use of that word from our pulpits in the last fifty or so years, the theory being that speaking of sin brings a sin-consciousness which causes man to sin. That almost sounds logical until you consider the flip side of that coin which dictates that silence on the matter will cause sin to languish in our vocabulary and eventually fade away. Ah, now we see the absurdity of that claim! Why did God send His only begotten Son to die on a cross? If sin could simply be ignored out of existence, why did blood flow down? The very idea violates the entirety of the Word of God, both letter and spirit.

IS THE CHURCH IN AMERICA LARGELY INEFFECTIVE TODAY BECAUSE OF THE DEPRAVED STATE OF OUR SOCIETY?

OR IS OUR SOCIETY IN THAT CORRUPT STATE BECAUSE THE CHURCH HAS BECOME LARGELY INEFFECTIVE?

Covetousness incognito

How has this revised thinking trickled down through the last few generations? What has been its impact in America? Apparently the Lord saw covetousness as a significant threat; after all, it was on His top ten list. Methodically dissecting that Tenth Commandment should help us trace the course of the river of impact, beginning at its source and ending with our appalling legacy to future generations. For the sake of clarity, let's repeat that passage one more time:

> *Exodus 20:17, "17 You shall not covet your neighbor's house; you shall not covet your neighbor's wife, nor his male servant, nor his female servant, nor his ox, nor his donkey, nor anything that is your neighbor's."*

1. *You shall not covet your neighbor's house.* As with each of the commands, what it says is exactly what it means; however, within the definition of the word translated "house" here we find that it includes not only the structure itself but everything contained within the dwelling. How do we rate on that one in America on a scale of one to ten? Make it more personal: how do you rate yourself?

Our visit to Eden at the point of temptation makes it clear to us that discontent is not necessarily related to money and possessions and houses and three-car garages and swimming pools and showers big enough to host a small dinner party.

1ˢᵗ Timothy 6:8, "⁸ And having food and raiment let us be therewith content."

Food and a roof over your head. Yikes! That just offends everything the American mind holds dear. In my younger days I experienced a rather lengthy time of intense, abject poverty. The place where my children and I lived was long overdue for condemnation but it was the best I could afford. The roof had leaked for so many years that mushrooms hung from the ceiling, dangling upside down in a weird sort of clothesline effect. Raw sewage flowed into an open field and the bathroom floor threatened to crumble under even the slightest weight. The thermostat would often top off above 100 degrees on summer days, forcing us to retreat outside to a little shade tree until the sun mercifully disappeared behind the treetops. I can remember cooking supper in that little kitchen, periodically dashing outside to cool off. We often ate our evening meal seated there on the ground.

Did God take pleasure in scrutinizing our discomfort? Was He indifferent to our poverty? Was He detached or withdrawn from the mother's tears that were shed under that leaky roof? To even entertain such thoughts would be an affront to His character as revealed to us in the Word.

Did He demand that I be satisfied to keep my babies in that deplorable place? Satisfied, no; content, yes. See the difference? One thing I learned during that period was this: It is a lot easier to be content when you have nothing and no way of acquiring things than it is when you have every need met. During those years of lack I learned to become totally dependent upon the Lord for the most basic necessities of life because I had no choice. Like Paul, I learned to live abased. There were countless hours after the babies were asleep where I cried out to the Lord for help and I can testify to you today that my children never, ever went hungry. By God's grace my babies not only survived but flourished as He gloriously made a way where there was no way from abasement to abundance. In that place I lived out Timothy's admonition, *"godliness with contentment is great gain,"* not by choice but by necessity. That is not God's best for us. True contentment emerges when God has entrusted us with more than enough and we still allow the Holy Spirit to train our hands to the reins of the tug of self-indulgence.

Do not covet your neighbor's house and all the stuff therein. There is always one newer, one bigger, one in a more prestigious neighborhood. Theirs will always be filled with newer, shinier trinkets. Retail marketers will see to that. Their whole reason for hauling out of bed in the morning is to find some way to convince us that we need that bigger and better widget in order to be happy. Witness the green shag carpet of the 70's? Where is it today? How about the avocado colored appliances that every kitchen needed in the late 60's? Seen one lately? Right now it is all about stainless steel. Everybody who is anybody has matching stainless steel appliances in the kitchen. Latest home décor flash? Stainless steel is on its way out and new shades of style are hitting the showrooms.

The list of potential carrots hovering just out of our reach is endless: cell phones, shoes, tools, automobiles, etc., and we might expect the world to traipse after such things, but what about us? What about the Christians in America? What are we teaching our children about contentment?

2. *You shall not covet your neighbor's wife.* The New Testament is filled with instruction concerning the marriage relationship and its proper observance. Jesus quoted from the great commandments here:

   Matthew 5:27-28, "[27]* You have heard that it was said to those of old, 'You shall not commit adultery.'* [28]* But I say to you that whoever looks at a woman to lust for her has already committed adultery with her in his heart."*

   Not only did Jesus uphold and reinforce the Old Testament ban on adultery, but He expanded our understanding of the Old Testament command by bringing our thought life into the equation. We cannot escape the fact that these words of our Lord were addressed to each and every one of us…. including us, ladies, but our purpose here is not to police your thought life. Instead, we need to focus on what the church is doing to teach His words and to reinforce His words and to set a standard in our own lives by His words.

   I would like to propose that we can take this particular element and carry it even one step further. Not only are we forbidden to covet the person of the spouse of our neighbor but we must avoid the pitfall of coveting the relationship that the two of them might share. This jealous craving for what we perceive as the fairytale relationship of others may cause us to sell our own marital commitment out for greener crabgrass. Gazing covetously at other relationships will soon cause vows to be forgotten and dreams to die before they ever see the light of day. It is this aspect of covetousness which has taken our nation (and the church) by storm, and it is that which we have bequeathed upcoming generations. We are chillingly close to birthing generations of men and women who quite simply do not understand what is so special about marriage and fidelity.

3. *You shall not covet his male servant or his female servant.* The mere employment of servants implies riches and wealth on the part of the master, but this statement does not necessarily direct our hearts back to wealth. Instead it evokes the idea of an entire lifestyle of affluence and maybe even decadent luxury. In the mid-1980's a television show called "Lifestyles of the Rich and Famous" exploded onto the scene. Week after week Robin Leach whisked us away from our ordinary lives and into the magical world of celebrity homes and holidays, leaving everyday families with a terminal case of jealousy, and always with his signature sign-off: "Champagne wishes and caviar dreams." The show is no longer broadcast other than possible syndication viewings, but the concept has remained. What we want most is what we cannot have. We have taught our children thoroughly. Unfortunately what we have taught and what we observe within the local church violates everything that the Bible teaches us about covetousness.

From rags to riches

I once had the honor and privilege of knowing a pastor whose great call was that of ministering to the downtrodden of society. The little storefront church was consistently filled with men and women who were alone in this world, homeless and hopeless, many desperately entangled with fierce addictions. Those who filled those old pews every Sunday had been broken and trampled so badly that you could almost see the bleeding of the wounds they bore. There was no pretense in that sanctuary, just genuine gratitude toward a very gracious and merciful Savior.

The heart of that that little gem of a flock became really clear to me one evening as I taught the Bible from that rickety pulpit. As I looked out over the crowd of maybe seventy or so I could see a distinctive line of demarcation between those who had been gloriously saved and delivered and those who were yet to experience the great salvation of the Lord. The latter's body language was fraught with tension, men and women squirming in anticipation of the end of the message, arms tightly crossed across chests as though that alone would shield them from the seducing love of God. The message concluded and the altar call was given; many people responded, but way in the back of the room there was one man who refused to stand with the rest of the congregation and instead remained rigid in his defensive posture with a scowl on his face. Eventually it was over; the service was done and people began to mill around and chat, but out of the corner of my eye I noticed that same man making his way very deliberately toward me. This could not be good, I thought. He was a very large hunk of a man, tall and broad, clothed in lots of leather set off by a red bandana and Khan moustache which coordinated well with his very long braided hair. You get the picture. He waited until I had finished with well-wishers and then he stepped up and announced his intent to clear something up. Thinking that no man would hurt an old woman, I said something like, "Yes, son, what can I do for you?" It was only then that I saw the tears welling up as he explained that he could not bring himself to stand in the sanctuary and sing and pray because he had done too many bad things; it was okay for other, holier, people, but not for him. He was concerned that I would take his non-participation as a personal affront and he was there to ask forgiveness from me. We had a wonderful time in the Lord that night, this wonderful man and I, as he began to grasp the height and depth of God's grace.

That man's bearing was fairly typical of that congregation as a whole in the beginning, but after a few years the people began to murmur and complain because they wanted to be like other congregations: nice pews, new carpet, shiny new instruments, and an arena-worthy sound system. What they did not want was dirty people tracking up the place, kids making too much noise in the services, and – God forbid – people smoking just outside the door. Their attitude of gratitude had changed to covetousness very quickly and the precious pastor was never able to restore the original vision of that work. He was summarily dismissed and a new, more relevant pastor was brought in. The entire work imploded within a short time.

All the accoutrements of American church life beckon. We have allowed the mega-church chapter in America to set unrealistic standards for congregations across the nation. Pastors and their leaders strive to meet the earthly expectations of their flock, of their city, and most despicably, other pastors. Everybody wants to be like the big guys, but at what price? Covetousness. And to what end? Offense to the most basic principles taught by Christ Himself.

4. Do not covet your neighbor's ox (or bull) or his donkey. These two mostly uninspiring but valuable creatures were instrumental in the occupational, religious, and practical lives of the Old Testament families. Great care was given in their policing since oxen have been known to throw their weight around now and then. (There's a reason they call those guys bullies, you know.) It

was common practice to twist and weave hay around the horns of overly bullish bulls as a warning to people to steer clear. (No pun intended.) The ox was used for food, as sacrifices, and as a worker in the fields. Remember when Elijah first met Elisha? Elisha was plowing with twenty-four oxen (or twelve yoke).[83]

The donkey was originally regarded as a wealthy man's mode of transport, but ultimately lost that distinction when they were replaced by horses. The donkey then came to be viewed as a part of the life of the poorer families. Remember Jesus' triumphal entry into Jerusalem?

These two utilitarian creatures represented the work life and social status of man, and so we might loosely re-state this command like this: Do not covet your neighbor's profession or occupation and the wealth or prestige that goes with it; do not covet the social standing or status that is his by virtue of his work.

5.   Do not covet anything that is your neighbor's. Now there is an all-encompassing command. If it is not yours, do not covet it. Be content.

Pluck out the root.

There you have it. Five spheres of potential temptation, and in the final analysis, covetousness is at the root of nearly all other sins. Was it not covetousness that was at the very root of the temptation in the wilderness? Jesus was hungry and so the temptation was first to covet bread and then to covet validation of His Deity, followed by the temptation to covet ease of life, relinquishing His destiny to the only shortcut which could spare the devil his own inevitable fate.

Have you and I been contributors to the neglect and decay of this stone of contentment in the church in America? Have we had a hand in bringing its hateful enticement right through the sanctuary doors? We now have a very usable gage with which to assess our own culpability, so let's do a quick appraisal:

1. Are we guilty of just never being content with our home and our possessions? Is there a constant compulsion to have bigger, better, and newer? Do we look at those around us through eyes of envy and even jealousy?

2. Are we guilty of discontent in our marriages? Do we look with envious eyes at other men and women? Do we covet relationships? Remember, this even includes your thought life. (Again, thank God for grace!)

3. Are we covetous of the lifestyle of others? Do we sometimes feel robbed of our rightful place of luxury?

4. Are we covetous of the professional life of others? Do we resent the wealth and/or social status associated with their careers?

5. Have we fallen prey to general discontent? Have we allowed that discontent to make its way into our church life?

Covetousness is largely an issue of perception; what is it that you perceive would satisfy your heart and allow you to be content? What is it in your life that robs you of the great prize of contentment?

The church in America at large has chosen to catalog sins, some being more tolerable than others in our eyes. There are the ones the world commits filed under sordid, repugnant, and disgusting; then there are the ones that we Christians want to keep around so we keep them in ready files entitled shortcomings or weaknesses. Shame on us.

Luke 1:76-79, "⁷⁶And thou, child, shalt be called the prophet of the Highest: for thou shalt go before the face of the Lord to prepare his ways; ⁷⁷To give knowledge of salvation unto his people by the remission of their sins, ⁷⁸Through the tender mercy of our God; whereby the dayspring from on high hath visited us, ⁷⁹To give light to them that sit in darkness and in the shadow of death, to guide our feet into the way of peace."

There are certain passages in the Word of God which instruct us very specifically, while others teach us of His person and His ways. Some guide His children through this earthly wilderness of soiled feet and polluted works, and others point to a celestial realm which we can only hope to know when we see Him face to face. Such is the passage above, an excerpt drawn from the song of Zacharias. It ascends to heights of grandeur, its lofty words speaking of spiritual things incomprehensible to the human mind. Tucked away in his song are these words, *"to guide our feet into the way of peace."* Peace, His transcendental peace, cannot rule where covetousness abides, and that dear friend is where we have fallen short. We have failed miserably in teaching our young adults, our teenagers, our tweens, our children, and our babies how to be content in the Lord. We have gone the way of the early false prophets who received a warning word through the Prophet Jeremiah:

Jeremiah 6:14, "¹⁴They have also healed the hurt (or the crushing) *of My people slightly* (or superficially), *Saying, 'Peace, peace!' When there is no peace."*

The prevailing message of our day leads us to get more from God by invoking His Word. More. More. Bigger. Shinier. Our children are pitching and rolling like a ship in a nor'easter; ferocious winds are driving the vessel of their lives where it will for no anchor is able to hold in such a storm save Christ Himself. The roar of the waves has deafened their ears, the driving rain has blinded them, and they are helpless to save themselves.

> *Romans 10:13-14, "[13] 'For whoever calls on the name of the Lord shall be saved.' [14] How then shall they call on Him in whom they have not believed? And how shall they believe in Him of whom they have not heard? And how shall they hear without a preacher?"*

But not just any preacher. How shall they hear without a preacher bearing the good news of the Gospel? How shall they hear that peace can be theirs and that His divine promises are more than enough? How can they believe it for themselves if the spiritual adults around them are seasick, too?

I implore you, dear friends, tell our children how to lash themselves to the mast of the Son of God in the midst of the storm.

CHAPTER 11

STONE NUMBER 11: CONSCIOUSNESS OF ETERNITY

The old preacher had put his heart and soul into the message that Sunday morning, calling out to his flock the raptures of heaven and dreadfulness of hell. The people, captivated by the prospect of both destinations, had listened raptly. Thinking to draw the net of his message, the preacher called out, "How many of you want to go to heaven?" Since only a fool would consciously choose the alternative, hands shot up all around the room with the exception of one little boy on the front row. So once again he cried out, "How many of you want to go to heaven?" He was puzzled when the boy's hands remained at his side. After the service was over, he asked the little boy, "Son, do you not want to go to heaven?" The boy was clearly surprised at the question. "Preacher," he explained, "I thought you were getting up a busload to go today."

If you have heard that old story before, odds are good that you are over fifty. If you are under the age of fifty you probably have not. It was a common preacher story decades ago, and its conspicuous absence in today's pulpits is no great loss; however, the lack of conversation concerning eternity is tragic.

Apostle Paul's writings were sometimes hard to grasp, but there was one specific occasion in which he communicated clearly and succinctly:

1ˢᵗ Corinthians 15:12-19, "¹²Now if Christ be preached that he rose from the dead, how say some among you that there is no resurrection of the dead? ¹³But if there be no resurrection of the dead, then is Christ not risen: ¹⁴And if Christ be not risen, then is our preaching vain, and your faith is also vain. ¹⁵Yea, and we are found false witnesses of God; because we have testified of God that he raised up Christ: whom he raised not up, if so be that the dead rise not. ¹⁶For if the dead rise not, then is not Christ raised: ¹⁷And if Christ be not raised, your faith is vain; ye are yet in your sins. ¹⁸Then they also which are fallen asleep in Christ are perished. ¹⁹If in this life only we have hope in Christ, we are of all men most miserable."

With the emergence of the great faith movement of recent decades came a calamitous halt in concern for things eternal. Our preoccupation with the affairs of this world has overshadowed the very existence of eternal life, but the truth of the matter is this: each of us will live eternally; only our destination has yet to be determined, and that by our personal redemption through the cross of Christ.

I am an old woman now; I was taught my spiritual heritage early on. I heard the old teachings Sunday in and Sunday out; I saw my parents live out their convictions in our home, and my life was formed and molded by all these when I was young. They kept me strong in the hardest of times, they comforted me in grievous days, and they called to me when I strayed from their voice. And now I wonder. I wonder what have I given my children, my grandchildren, and my great-grandchildren that will comfort and hold them? What have we – the church in America – given our children that will take them through the storm clouds on the horizon?

I can recall the bomb drills of my youth in school. Maybe some of you will recall how we were taught to get under our desks and cover our heads. In hindsight, I am pretty certain that would have done little to save us but it was something anyway. People were building underground bunkers and stockpiling supplies. Fear was rampant.

> IS THE CHURCH IN AMERICA LARGELY INEFFECTIVE TODAY BECAUSE OF THE DEPRAVED STATE OF OUR SOCIETY?
>
> OR IS OUR SOCIETY IN THAT CORRUPT STATE BECAUSE THE CHURCH IS LARGELY INEFFECTIVE?

In the face of apocalyptic fears of that day, churches across America stepped forward boldly and preached hope of salvation and expectation of better days to come. The saved and the unsaved reaped the benefits of sermons and teachings which testified of a loving and forgiving God, one who could and would respond to our prayers and petitions. Not everyone ran to the Lord, but every person was affected by the preaching of the cross and its benefits. Not everyone believed, but even the scoffer found some modicum of comfort in the truth that this world is not all there is. Our society was balanced out in its perspective because the Church was effective in its balanced message, but that was then and this is now. Now is tough. Now is treacherous. Now our young people get up every morning and walk into war zones called schools, and what they face every day cannot even be comprehended by someone from my generation. Since I began writing this exhortation, I have become hypersensitive to the young people around me, so much so that it often moves me to tears. I find myself voicing unheard apologies to them as I pass them on the street. "I am sorry, honey. I am sorry we have given you a heritage of confusion and hopelessness. I am sorry we have handed you a nation of unbelief." Our young men have no place to turn to find their God-given identity and in their earnest search to satisfy that deep rooted need, they have settled for counterfeit images. It is a painful thing to see. Our daughters are defenseless against the debauchery, exposed to every evil force seeking to destroy them. A friend and I recently stopped at a local video store to return a movie and there on the sidewalk sat a young girl in her very early teens. Her clothing was strategically cut (either by hand or by manufacture) to expose her young body. Her posture was typical of the daughters of our society, cast down and uncertain, casting uneasy glances in every direction, and I wept. I wept for all the girls who are adrift in the sea of our apathy; I wept for the lost among America's young people, lost for lack of knowledge; I wept because it is not just the world's daughters who are adrift but generations of precious souls who sit in our churches every week. *If in this life only we have hope in Christ, we are of all men most miserable.*

Back to the mountain

Return with me for a moment to the scene on Mount Carmel. As you will recall, the dilapidated state of the old altar was due neither to some military campaign nor to Jezebel's anti-Jehovah crusade but instead was the result of extended carelessness and disregard of God's own people. That is precisely what has happened in the Church in America. We can point fingers in the world's direction to make ourselves feel better, but the truth is that we are the ones who bear the burden of responsibility for throwing out a lifeline to a lost world.

> *Acts 20:26-27, "²⁶Wherefore I take you to record this day, that I am pure from the blood of all men. ²⁷For I have not shunned to declare unto you all the counsel of God."*

One remarkable commonality emerges among all the altar stones and that is this: our failure to preach the whole counsel of God has not been a passive act but a hostile one which has, however unintentionally, birthed arrogance among its subscribers with condescension toward those who fail to join in. For instance, I have heard the following statement made repeatedly over the past two decades: "Some people sing about the sweet bye and bye but I am more concerned about the now and now." Such quirky quips may bring quick and enthusiastic response from the congregation but they also cast aspersions on those Christians who hold tightly to a knowledge and anticipation of life in His presence, intimating that they are somehow just not quite as spiritual, that somehow they just don't get it. "Those people who look for a 'Mansion over the Hilltop' just do not understand the deeper things of God," they say. A dear friend of ours recently lost her husband quite unexpectedly and in preparing the memorial service she selected the song "The Eastern Gate," a long-time classic of eternal anticipation:

> Keep your lamps all trimmed and burning;
> For the Bridegroom watch and wait;
> He'll be with us at the meeting
> Just inside the Eastern Gate.[84]

Sadly, our friend was unable to take comfort in those words because she was unable to find a musician who even knew of the song. Our music is now devoid of references to eternity, our sermons seemingly oblivious to the existence of eternal destiny. Perhaps we have subscribed to the same erroneous mindset as pertains to sin: if we do not talk about it, it will go away. So what then, if we do not talk about eternity then maybe we can get away without making a choice? Absurd.

Jesus spoke warmly and passionately of that day both in parables and in first person:

> *John 17:24-26, "[24]Father, I will that they also, whom thou hast given me, be with me where I am; that they may behold my glory, which thou hast given me: for thou lovedst me before the foundation of the world. [25]O righteous Father, the world hath not known thee: but I have known thee, and these have known that thou hast sent me. [26]And I have declared unto them thy name, and will declare it: that the love wherewith thou hast loved me may be in them, and I in them."*

And why not? Heaven is described as a place of great joy and gladness, a place where we will dwell in His glorious presence in peace and rest:

> 1st Peter 1:6-8, "6 Wherein ye greatly rejoice, though now for a season, if need be, ye are in heaviness through manifold temptations: 7That the trial of your faith, being much more precious than of gold that perisheth, though it be tried with fire, might be found unto praise and honour and glory at the appearing of Jesus Christ: 8 Whom having not seen, ye love; in whom, though now ye see him not, yet believing, ye rejoice with joy unspeakable and full of glory:"

Joy unspeakable. Believe it or not, that joy unspeakable speaks of the joy we should be experiencing right now, here on earth. How much greater then will be our rejoicing when we are with Him where He is, beholding the fullness of His glory? And how shall the world know of such joy if we remain silent?

> 1st Thessalonians 5:1-3, "1But of the times and the seasons, brethren, ye have no need that I write unto you. 2For yourselves know perfectly that the day of the Lord so cometh as a thief in the night. 3For when they shall say, Peace and safety; then sudden destruction cometh upon them, as travail upon a woman with child; and they shall not escape."

I doubt that there are many who would dispute the fact that we are living in the last of the last days. Our world is awash in the very narrative prophetic words of Jesus Himself, words such as these: Many will declare that there is more than one way to God; there will be wars and rumors of wars; nation will rise against nation; there will be famines, pestilences, and earthquakes; false prophets will arise from every quarter; there will be a preoccupation with self-indulgence;

marriage would be taken as lightly as dust in the wind. "*Watch*," Jesus said, "*for you do not know what hour your Lord is coming.*"[85] A thief in the night. Suddenly. In the twinkling of an eye. Those kinds of descriptive words should send chills of awe down the spine of us all, even the saved, for who can fathom the splendor and the wonder of the sights of that day?

There is an oft-quoted passage found in 1st Peter, renowned for its final six words, but we do that passage an injustice when we slide right past the first part and that which follows:

> *1st Peter 2:24-25, "24Who his own self bare our sins in his own body on the tree, that we, being dead to sins, should live unto righteousness: <u>by whose stripes ye were healed</u>.*
> *25For ye were as sheep going astray; but are now returned unto the Shepherd and Bishop of your souls."*

He bore our sins on the tree (literally on the wood of the cross of Calvary) so that you and I could face these last days unafraid and ultimately stand justified before Him clothed in His righteousness. We were as dumb sheep, deceived and wandering aimlessly in our sin, but now we are heirs of God, joint heirs with Christ; we are led, protected, and guarded by the Great Shepherd, the Bishop of our souls. What soothing and comforting words, and yet, we need not think that we will march ourselves into His presence as though we were bellying up to the counter at the local fast food restaurant, demanding recognition. God forbid!

And what of the unsaved man or woman? "*And if the righteous scarcely be saved, where shall the ungodly and the sinner appear?*"[86] Who can conceive of the terror of that court date before the throne of God? Who can even imagine the dread in the heart of our unsaved friends and neighbors when they face the stark realization that there truly is an eternity and there indeed is a judgment and there really is a God on a very real throne issuing forth very real judgments? The door will be closed. It will be too late.

There must be a remedy

We cannot force the world to accept Christ. Had that been even remotely possible, I have known some hard-preaching evangelists who would have had the job done by now. We will not be held accountable for the whole world but we will be held accountable for what we knew to do and refused. We are a nation of anguished souls searching for relief and hope in idolatrous worship, in promiscuous relationships, in illicit drugs and pharmaceuticals, in clawing our way to the top of the worldly ladder of success, and in possessing worldly goods. Our nation is very much like the description of man found in the 107th Psalm: *"26 ..... their soul is melted because of trouble. 27 They reel to and fro, and stagger like a drunken man, and are at their wits' end."*

That aptly describes you and me before we surrendered our life to Christ, but someone somewhere told us of a new and different way through the blood of the cross. Who will tell our tormented nation of eternal hope?

> *Psalm 107:28-30, "28 Then they cry unto the LORD in their trouble, and he bringeth them out of their distresses. 29 He maketh the storm a calm, so that the waves thereof are still. 30 Then are they glad because they be quiet; so he bringeth them unto their desired haven."*

What is the remedy? Restore a keen consciousness of eternal destination to the repertoire of the church. Make no mistake, you will face opposition but it is unlikely that anyone will place a crown of thorns on your head or nail you to a cross or pierce your side. Stand strong even in the face of ridicule and scorn and teach that there is a heaven and there is a hell; teach of His great sacrifice so that we might dwell with Him forever. Preach. Teach. Warn. Counsel. It took decades for the enemy of God to remove a consciousness of eternity from its rightful place in church teachings; restoring it will require a tireless, diligent effort on the part of pastors, leaders, and teachers.

And the next time you see a young person about town that seems lost on the stormy sea of hopelessness and despair, when you look into his or her eyes and see the loneliness of a disposable generation, maybe you too will be moved to weep. Maybe the Lord will allow you to say to that one, "Please forgive me, dear child. I am so sorry. There are a few things we forgot to tell you."

CHAPTER 12

STONE NUMBER 12: IDENTITY CRISIS

We are all familiar with the electrifying story of the imprisonment of Paul and Silas and how mightily God moved as they sang and prayed their way through the captivity. We do love those Bible stories that excite us and cause us to stand and clap or shout with joy, and that particular passage likely ranks in the top ten in that respect, but it is not the hip-hip hooray part of that passage that calls to us now. Instead, throw it in reverse and back up to these verses:

> *Acts 16:16-17, "⁶ Now it happened, as we went to prayer, that a certain slave girl possessed with a spirit of divination met us, who brought her masters much profit by fortune-telling. ¹⁷ This girl followed Paul and us, and cried* (screaming and shrieking) *out, saying, 'These men are the servants of the Most High God, who proclaim to us the way of salvation.'"*

Were they not the servants of the Most High God? Did they not proclaim the way of salvation to all who would hear? Yes on both counts and so what drove Paul to take command so authoritatively? The Bible goes on to tell us that even though the words were true, the spirit behind the words were demonic. In other words Satan took a truth and tweaked it just enough to draw attention away from the God's absoluteness. Day after day this girl (under demonic influence) followed Paul and Silas around, not just speaking mind you but screaming and shrieking these same words. Can you imagine the chaos that would have caused? I would imagine that many folks turned away from Paul and Silas just to escape the presence of this disruptive slave girl. There is certainly no way that Paul and Silas could have articulated the truth of the gospel clearly with such distraction and interference.

Stolen identity

In similar fashion, the church in America has fallen prey to one of its most common axioms which goes something like this: You will never reach your potential in God's kingdom until you realize who you are in Christ. Is that not a true statement? Is it not the truth to the very depth of its content? Yes on both counts and so what is the problem? It is actually twofold:

1. The motivation behind the phrase is too often rooted in getting what we want from God by using His own Word to create an unfailing formula. The Bible is resplendent with promises from the throne of God to His people, but our motivations and agendas can quickly pollute that lifeline.

2. The second is actually the more relevant to our study. The continual crying out of these words has drowned out the wholeness and cohesiveness of the Bible. As a result we have made it nearly impossible for those around us who are bruised and broken (both saved and unsaved) to find their way to comfort and refuge in His love.

Let's examine those words once again: You will never reach your potential in God's kingdom until you realize who you are in Christ. As stated, most all of us would give a hearty amen at this point, so how do we put it into practice in the fullness of its intent? That one question leads us to the final altar stone: the stone of identity.

The humble onion

For illustrative purposes, let us turn to the humble onion. The onion is composed of several closely held but loosely bonded concentric layers, but it is an onion through and through. Every layer looks like an onion, smells like an onion, triggers weeping like an onion, and flavors like an onion. Whole, sliced, diced, julienned, chopped, or juiced….it is still an onion. We batter them and call them bloomin', we ring them and serve them with dip, we throw them on burgers, drown them with ketchup, savor them in soups, and enjoy them in the cuisine of nearly every ethnicity on this globe. But they are still onions.

We could take a lesson. Elijah acknowledged the same truth that day on Mount Carmel. His prayer would probably be viewed with disdain in the U. S. churches of today, seen as theologically lacking. As we have the translation of Elijah's prayer, it consists of sixty-three little words. Why, that's hardly enough to make two or three positive confessions. Nonetheless the power of God fell and Elijah's story made history forever. Inside of those few words, Elijah acknowledged who God was (His Divine, Omnipotent identity) and he set apart and confirmed (or identified) the Israelites on the basis of the patriarchs with whom God had made covenant. Remember these were not just a few Israelites scattered around on that mount but rather a multitude and their numbers likely included businessmen, carpenters, farmers, sheepherders, cooks, fishermen, open air market hawkers, and all the other secular assignments of their society, but the prayer was not made on that basis. Instead, it was based on the most elementary, the central core of who they were: the people of God. To this day, Jews are globally recognized by that same rudimentary, basic identity. After that, they may be known as bankers, businessmen, housewives, and professional men and women in every imaginable work, but when you peel that onion back, they are still Jews.

What does that say about us? Like our earlier example, let's climb a new mountain, one which will allow us to look back critically onto the peak of accepted thought. On the way up, let's meditate on how people know you and what they know about you. Do they immediately say, "He/She is a Christian first and foremost."? Or would they have to wander through a maze of other identifiers before *maybe* remembering that you are a Christian? Or would they know that at all? Bear in mind that we are speaking not only of your immediate or extended family, your close friends, or your circle of casual acquaintance. Widen your self-examination to casual contacts: unacquainted neighbors, store clerks, underpaid struggling workers in the drive-thru windows, and the driver in the lane next to you. Are we at the summit and ready to shine the light?

Did you reach some conclusions about your own identity? Are you a disciple of Christ first and foremost? What is your primary identity in your own mind? That is a critical question because that is where your identity comprehension begins. You may find that your spiritual identity is secondary even within your own consciousness. Do you see yourself as a husband or wife first and then allow all other perceptions to flow from that identity or do you see yourself in light of your occupation, a man or woman who happens also to be an artist, an athlete, a father or mother, or a myriad of other identifiers? To bring these questions into a more narrow focus, do you view your discipleship as the nucleus of your identity or as simply another descriptive signpost to define who you are?

What is your primary identity in the eyes of others? No one (least of all a Christian) should birth or bear an identity simply for the sake of public opinion. Nonetheless, how others see us can be quite revealing. As always, the Bible is our only sure source and so let's take a look at a few of the Bible's notable characters:

1. Consider David. This king was renowned throughout the kingdom even before he ascended to the throne. What was it

that drew people to David? Why were they singing songs about David when he was but a servant to King Saul? It was not because of all the positive character traits of David, nor did he campaign throughout the kingdom for followers. It was his core identity: the anointed man of God. In spite of all the pomp and glory that would become his, David's core self-realization found its source in the Lord. The Psalms are filled with confirmations of his right identity:

Psalms 24:8-10, "⁸Who is this King of glory? The LORD strong and mighty, the LORD mighty in battle. ⁹Lift up your heads, O ye gates; even lift them up, ye everlasting doors; and the King of glory shall come in. ¹⁰Who is this King of glory? The LORD of hosts, he is the King of glory. Selah."

2. Rahab gave us a glimpse into the core identity of the Israelites:

    Joshua 2:11, "¹¹And as soon as we had heard these things, our hearts did melt, neither did there remain any more courage in any man, because of you: for the LORD your God, he is God in heaven above, and in earth beneath."

    Their reputation had spread far and wide, not because of what they had done, but because of who they were, and since who they were found its root in the one true God, the world took note.

3. How about the woman with the alabaster box? No great fuss is made about her identity or credentials. Instead Jesus told those who loved religion to leave the woman alone. *"She has done what she could….."*[87] And what she did was to give a visual demonstration of her love for the Savior without inhibition or shame. As a result of her walking in her core identity, her story is *"told as a memorial"* even to this day and will continue to be told so long as the sun rises in the east.

We could go on and on; the list is endless, but we would be remiss if we did not test this truth against the life of Jesus. As would be expected, Jesus walked out this truth flawlessly; His acts were perfect, his motivation pure. Isn't it interesting that His miraculous, inexplicable deeds appealed to everyone but the religious folks? They only had an interest in discrediting Him by bringing into question His core identity.

Have you been allowing the Holy Spirit to examine your heart? What did you discover about yourself? Do you need to change some thought patterns?

Watch out for the goat!

There must be some well hidden rule somewhere that forbids laughter and mirth on Sunday mornings, but some of the world's greatest humor can be found around the halls and classrooms of the local church. Kids are spectacular when it comes to that. I read years ago about one little boy who described Lot's wife as "a pillar of salt by day and a ball of fire by night." We recently experienced one of those bloopers at my home church. The person who was in charge of the projection of announcements, Scriptures, etc., had mis-posted the title of that day's sermon. It read, "I need to slay some goats in my life." I always like to try to figure out the text or the direction of the sermon, and I decided this one must draw from the Old Testament scapegoat and so I anxiously waited for the goat sermon. As it turned out, it should have read, "I need to slay some giants in my life." Everyone had a good chuckle and our pastor proceeded to preach an amazing giant-slaying message. In the process he asked the question, "What is your giant?" I was amazed to find that my giant actually *was* a goat, the scapegoat of the Old Testament. The high priest, having offered the sacrifices associated with the Day of Atonement, would lay his hands upon the head of the scapegoat, thereby conferring the sins of the nation upon the goat. The scapegoat was then ushered into the wilderness by a specifically designated man. In a sense then, the sinful identity of the nation rode on the head of that scapegoat. The man who led that goat into the wilderness was considered unclean which necessitated a process of purification before he could return to camp. Such is the case with us, but let's confine our examination to the issue of our identity:

> Romans 6:6-11, "*⁶Knowing this, that our old man is crucified with him, that the body of sin might be destroyed, that henceforth we should not serve sin. ⁷For he that is dead is freed from sin. ⁸Now if we be dead with Christ, we believe that we shall also live with him: ⁹Knowing that Christ being raised from the dead dieth no more; death hath no more dominion over him. ¹⁰For in that he died, he died unto sin once: but in that he liveth, he liveth unto God. ¹¹Likewise reckon ye also yourselves to be dead indeed unto sin, but alive unto God through Jesus Christ our Lord.*"

Our identifier, the most basic categorization of who we are, is now found in Him. That's what the Bible says. The Achilles heel for most Christians is our affinity for that disgusting goat in the wilderness. We persist in searching the desert wasteland for our pet goat, not so much for acts of sin, but for identification, of self-realization, and actuation.

Maybe a couple of examples will make this point clearer. Let's start with me. I am the daughter of two amazing parents. I am a single mother, grandmother, and great grandmother. I worked very, very hard to raise my children and I made more mistakes than one can even imagine, but by His grace we made it through. I worked for the DoD for some thirty years. I was ordained into the work of the ministry in 1992, well into my middle aged years. Having said all of that, who I am can be reduced to these few words: I am a disciple of Christ. That is what people should see.

Those Christians who have attained great academic and professional achievement and received accolades in high circles may have even more difficulty with this concept. These folks would have invested years of intense study, sacrificing socially, academically, physically, and monetarily and so their desire to be thus recognized is understandable, and yet the greatest of all their achievements is to be "*dead with Christ.*" They are His disciples.

Let's go to the other extreme. There is a slice of American society which is quite literally abused: those who fell along the roadside. We cannot say that they are forgotten for our media keeps them forever before our eyes, often to further personal agendas, nor can we call them lost because we pass them on the street every day, either averting our eyes or tossing a few coins their way to salve our consciences. Politicians use them as bargaining chips, the church hopes they just go away, and society seems determined to perpetuate their helplessness, but sometimes these wonderful people run headlong into the saving grace of our Lord and immediately they are on level ground with every other Christian. They become "*dead with Christ.*" They become His disciples.

Why is this change in mindset so important? It is important because the Bible says it is important:

> *John 12:23-26,* "*²³And Jesus answered them, saying, The hour is come, that the Son of man should be glorified. ²⁴Verily, verily, I say unto you, Except a corn of wheat fall into the ground and die, it abideth alone: but if it die, it bringeth forth much fruit. ²⁵He that loveth his life shall lose it; and he that hateth his life in this world shall keep it unto life eternal. ²⁶If any man serve me, let him follow me; and where I am, there shall also my servant be: if any man serve me, him will my Father honour.*"

Jesus was speaking, of course, of His impending crucifixion, burial, and resurrection, but since we are "*dead with Christ*" then it follows that the same principle applies to us. We are continuously amazed that the harvest in America is so unbelievably difficult, but the principle of seed and harvest is at work here. "*Except a corn of wheat fall into the ground and die, it abideth alone; but if it die, it bringeth forth much fruit.*" We are not who we were; we are not even who we see that we are. We are disciples of Christ.

> Colossians 3:1-3, *"If ye then be risen with Christ, seek those things which are above, where Christ sitteth on the right hand of God. ²Set your affection on things above, not on things on the earth. ³ For ye are dead, and your life is hid with Christ in God."*

You are dead (that is the seed) and your life and all that it holds is hidden with Christ in God. The very first thing people should see when they come into contact with you is Jesus and therefrom comes the harvest.

Jesus was very, very good at answering a simple question with an unfathomable reply. In John 12:20-21, we read of some Greeks who had requested an audience with Jesus. Philip of Bethsaida told Andrew who told Philip the disciple who relayed the message to Jesus. The above verses are taken from Jesus' response. Do you see anything in those verses that answers the Greeks' request? Ah, but it does. Jesus does not draw the net until we get to Verse 32:

> John 12:32, *"³²And I, if I be lifted up from the earth, will draw all men unto me."*

In other words, when this corn of wheat (Jesus) had fallen to the ground He would yield a multitude of like corns (you and me) and through the resultant proliferous harvest of corns, every man, woman, boy, and girl would be drawn to Him through the work of the Holy Spirit. There would be no need to make an appointment to see and touch Jesus for those "like corns" would be readily available all around. The condition is that those corns must die to all other identities and live as disciples of Christ who just happen to be doctors and administrators and blue collar workers, etc.

The benefits of recovered identity

Great principle with great promise, is it not? But it is also a very practical principle. There are some certain immediate benefits from this settling of identity:

Kinship among Christians would skyrocket. I am habitually up and ready to start the day before the sun rises. (That is not a braggartly thing to say. I am simply a morning person. By 1:00 p.m. I am completely useless.) On one recent morning the temperature was so agreeable that we were able to throw open the windows and breathe some fresh air. As I sat down before my computer I could hear the glorious tolling of the bells of the local St. Vincent de Paul Catholic Church. I have heard these bells calling to our town since I was a child. You can hear them throughout our smallish town and even beyond, out into the countryside farms and I marveled that every person who heard that sound knew precisely where it came from and what the pealing represented. The sound which resonates from that bell tower calls to the world at large that Christ has risen, that there is hope in a world ravaged by darkness. They chime to the Catholic, to the Protestant, to the saved and the unsaved alike. The bells do not discriminate. Honed in on our common core identity perhaps we Christians could manage to be a little nicer to one another.

I have known a very few people who were so given over to dispensing the love and grace of God that people were drawn to them like magnets. They have managed to grasp the corn of wheat concept and, wonder of wonders, it worked. Those around us, and especially the younger generation need to see us greet one another with genuine warmth as people of kindred spirit.

There is something in the created make-up of mankind that is captivated by the idea of a rallying point. We all want to be part of something larger than ourselves. We certainly saw this in the story of the Tower of Babel. Denominational labels often become rallying points to the congregants as do their unique, time-honored practices. One might assemble in great cathedrals while another sees a call to street-level storefront; some use instruments in their worship services while others adhere strictly to the voices of the people harmonizing strong and clear. There are those who place great emphasis upon the physical appearance while others leave that to the conscience of the people, for better or for worse. One might be known for their high decibel preaching while others teach quietly and methodically. The one common point for us all is this: *"For ye are dead, and your life is hid with Christ in God."* That gives us a rallying point of commonality and a launching pad for the future because, make no mistake, the world is watching and listening.

And finally, seeing ourselves first and foremost as disciples of Christ gives us the ability to prefer one another.

Romans 12:10, "¹⁰Be kindly affectioned one to another with brotherly love; in honour preferring one another;"

Jesus clearly placed love at the root of every act of life. This particular verse is tucked away amidst twelve other love-charging verses. It speaks to our leading the way for the honor of others. Only a person who truly grasps their identity in Christ can do that for the old nature craves recognition and notoriety. The idea of preferring the success and honor of someone else above and beyond our own stature is completely foreign to the flesh. The flesh will honor someone else gladly.... so long as they stay one step below us. However, a corn of wheat which has fallen to the ground and died has no problem with preferring others.

This particular benefit of core identity might most universally be recognizable in this setting: Pastors, leaders, and laity across this nation pray for a move of revival in the land that we all love so dearly. We fast. We assemble and pray. We pray in our prayer closets and we wait. We wait for it to happen in *our* church. God forbid that the Lord show up in power and might down the street or across town or – horror of horrors – in a congregation that believes a little differently than we do. Dead corns of wheat do not think that way.

The placement of this altar stone of identity in the teachings of the church of America will discourage fence dwellers. I am guessing that every pastor knows that term. Elijah was familiar with it as well:

> *1ˢᵗ Kings 18:21, "²¹And Elijah came unto all the people, and said, How long halt ye between two opinions? if the LORD be God, follow him: but if Baal, then follow him. And the people answered him not a word."*

How long? How many more Sundays will we walk into the sanctuary determined to make Almighty God fit into our frame? How many more services will we walk out as defeated and as empty as when we entered? How long will it take for Christians to pick up the torch of the gospel to bear light to a nation which is in desperate trouble? How long can we choose to ignore the decayed state of our nation and how long can we persist in our denial of responsibility?

Read the headlines. Actually read them. You will have to make a concentrated effort to do so because we are shell-shocked, shockproof. Read them. Face up to the mess we are leaving to our kids and our grandkids and generations to come. It is not hopeless; it does not have to worsen, but we must agree that politicians cannot solve our problems for us, the court system cannot make it all go away by decree, and philanthropists cannot pay us out of this morass. The turning point will come when we Christians begin to put into practice the words we have spoken for years: we will learn who we are in Christ, not for our own gain but for the sake of generations to come.

> *John 13:35, "³⁵By this all will know that you are My disciples, if you have love one for another."*

CONCLUSION
HERE COMES THE RAIN!

The contention of this entire written exhortation can be found in this thought: The altar on Mount Carmel had become nothing more than a hapless pile of rocks because of the neglect and carelessness of the people of God. They had found comfort for the flesh in the surrounding culture and had no real interest in changing. Consider Elijah's very deliberate actions that day:

- He openly mocked the prophets of Baal.
- He called all the people to gather round.
- He meticulously carried the altar stones, making a point to restore one per tribe, testifying to the covenant with the entire nation.
- He made a trench.
- He carefully placed the wood.
- He prepared the bull and laid it on the wood.
- He ordered four waterpots filled with water to be poured upon the sacrifice and the wood.
- He ordered a second round of waterpots filled with water to be dispensed likewise.
- He ordered yet a third round of waterpots to be emptied upon the sacrifice and the wood.
- He filled the trench with water.

That may seem a little on the theatrical order, but Elijah was no fool; he knew that his first challenge was to capture the eyes and ears of the Israelites. He also knew that God had his back, so to speak, and so he kept that water coming. It was common practice among the heathen to conceal fire in a pit dug under the sacrifice and altars of idols, giving the impression that fire had fallen on the sacrifice. This soaking of the sacrifice and the wood assured the people that what they were about to see was straight from the one true God of Israel.

As events unfolded, the fire of the Lord fell, consuming the sacrifice, the wood, the stones, and the dust and even licked up the water that was in the trench, and the people jumped off the fence and fell to the ground declaring, *"The Lord, He is God! The Lord, He is God!"* But our exhortation falls short if we stop there because it still had not rained, and it is refreshing, life-giving rain that America needs today.

Elijah had confidence that the drought would end because he had made proper preparation. What if Elijah had gone to Mount Carmel at his own presumptive prompting, looked to heaven, and cried out, "In the name of Jehovah God, come, rain."? What if he had failed to make proper preparation? Would God have sent the rain? Ahab had ordered that the children of Israel gather there on Mount Carmel at Elijah's command, but that did not happen in five minutes or ten or thirty. Slowly but surely the people made the trek, stopping within eyesight of the decayed altar of Jehovah God, a pitiful testimony to their neglect. Each man who made that journey was forced to gaze upon what his own carelessness had wrought and yet not one man among them gives us any hint of repentance or sorrow. Perhaps it was that stony callousness which prompted Elijah to cry out, *"How long will you falter between two opinions?"*

We know that Elijah had executed this scene by direction of the Lord Himself for we read in his prayer, *".....and that I have done all these things at Your word."* The coming of rain was a vital slice of God's word to Elijah. It would be easy to get caught up in the drama there on Mount Carmel for it is full of relatable scenes, but if we allow our minds to dwell upon those things, we miss the whole point at hand.

Remember that while the called assembly, the prophets' confrontation, the restoration of the altar stones, and the meticulous preparation of the altar proper set the stage for a demonstration of the power of God, it was the rain that the people needed.....life giving and sustaining rain. Of what value would the hyperbole have been if the whole event failed to produce rain? And so Elijah began to pray. He did not offer up a prayer for rain until preparation had been made, but after. Right order. And that, dear brothers and sisters, is our charge today.

I have been around long enough to know that there are many, many pastors, leaders, and laity who sense the desperate need for a spiritual revival in America, a nation dying of spiritual thirst. There are prayer meetings taking place across our nation, corporate fasts have become commonplace. Our motives are right, our intents pure and yet our nation sinks deeper and deeper into its state of hopelessness and despair. Just a few days ago, a very good friend described that state as implosion, a nation collapsing inward by its own hand, an apt description and a very scary one. That brings us back to our original question:

Is the Church in America largely ineffective today because of the depraved state of our society?

Or is our society in that corrupt state because the Church is largely ineffective?

We can no longer afford to live in denial, fellow Christians. The time has come to face the truth. We are the ones who have failed our nation because we have turned away from the whole Word of God. We have lost our salty flavor and put a basket over our light.

1. The fear of God has been replaced with carless familiarity.

2. Salvation has been replaced by many paths to God eastern mysticism.

3. The Bible has been replaced with revisionist doctrine.

4. Sacrificial consecration has been carefully tucked away by inattention, replaced by the world system of climbing the spiritual corporate ladder.

5. Fervent prayer has been replaced with positive thinking and carefully crafted utterances.

6. Commitment to a local body of believers has given way to a constant migration, dependent upon who offers the most prolific smorgasbord of benefits.

7. Faithful attendance, fellowship, and loyalty to the house of God have been subjected to a presumed leeward grace.

8. Mutual respect has been assaulted by gossip, backbiting, judgmental attitudes, and competitive tendencies, eating away at relationships among us to the point that trust among us has failed.

9. Marriage and family, as delineated in the Bible, has been replaced by teachings of tolerance. Unyielding teachings concerning marriage and family are viewed as harsh and uncaring, and yet the present state of marriage and family has produced behavior which can only be described as barbaric. There were nineteen children killed in the horrific Oklahoma City bombing in 1995, a disgraceful stain upon our nation, but that figure is dwarfed by the number of children who die at the hand of a parent, week in and week out in this nation.

10. Rest and contentment has been replaced by swirls of activity. Busy, busy, busy.

11. The consciousness of eternity has been replaced by the get-get-get mindset of this life and all it has to offer.

12. Open identification as a Christian is disdained and is, in fact, becoming perilous.

The forecast says rain.

Elijah faced a situation that was bleak by all definition. When he went to Mount Carmel he was painfully aware that if God failed to show up in all His power and His might, he would be publicly humiliated and stripped of his reputation among the people, but Elijah had been given a glimpse of the mind of God. Not only would the God of Abraham, Isaac, and Israel be present, but ....once order had been established.... so would the rain.

There are dozens of ways our nation may fall; there is but one way for it to rise to greatness, and His name is Jesus. It is not too late; America has a bright future so long as there remains a remnant of people who are willing to press forward in the power of the Holy Spirit. Will we get this ship righted overnight? Absolutely not, but we can begin. We can start. Will we get it right the first try? I doubt it, but we can say as Thomas Edison once said of his first tin foil phonograph, *"I was never so taken aback in my life – I was always afraid of things that worked the first time."*

I cannot improve upon the following commentary taken from the Full Life Study Bible:

> *Ephesians 6:17, "17And take the helmet of salvation, and the sword of the Spirit, which is the word of God;"*

"The sword of the Spirit, which is the word of God is the believer's offensive weapon to be used in his war against the power of evil. For this reason Satan will make every effort to undermine or destroy the Christian's confidence in that Word. The church must defend the inspired Scriptures against allegations that it is not God's Word in everything it teaches. To abandon the position and attitude of Christ and the apostles toward God's inspired Word is to destroy its power to convict or correct, to redeem, to heal, to drive out demons, and to overcome all evil. To deny its absolute trustworthiness in all it teaches is to deliver ourselves into the hand of Satan."[88]

How will history record the spiritual influence of the American church in our age? Will we be remembered as a kind and loving people or as folks who were more interested in grand buildings and ubiquitous programs? Will the writers of history note deeds of His mighty power or speak of abysmal self-absorption? Will they remember us as welcoming and kind-hearted or as an exclusionary private club? History rests on our shoulders. Yours and mine.

The upcoming generations are reaping the whirlwind of our neglect. Try this exercise. Sit down in front of network television one night from 8:00 to 11:00 p.m. Force yourself to watch it. Don't watch it for entertainment; watch it from a child's point of view. Watch it with the idea that all you are seeing is the truth. They do. Watch it even though it becomes painful. Do not close your eyes. Do not turn away. It should break your heart.

Try another test. Go to a mall or some other public area where people under thirty are known to gather. Watch them. Look at their faces. Observe their body language. Listen to their speech. Weep for them. Weep for the legacy we have bequeathed to them. Weep for the pressures that haunt them. Weep for the pharmaceuticals that they cling to just to get through life. Weep for a nation that has lost its way. And then go home. Go home and fall to your knees in repentance. Cry out to God for our young people. Seek Him with weeping for our precious teenagers, adrift in a turbulent sea desperately clinging to the leaky raft of intellectualism and humanism. Call to Him for the sweet little children who know nothing of His grace.

The old-time Pentecostals had a phrase which has nearly vanished from our lexicon. They called it "praying through." New theology disdains that practice, but I believe it is time to bring it back and give it a new title. Let's call it "praying until you get through." Let us stay on our knees in communion with God until we find release. Let us stay there until we have been drained of every ounce of our own strength. When we run out of words, let's pray in the Spirit. Let us kneel or stand; let us lay prostrate or jump and shout; let us be unstoppable in our pursuit of Him; let us go before Him again and again and again. And then when we are completely emptied, when we have captured His heart for His people, and when we are drained of self and alive to Christ let us rise up with a shout of victory and turn this nation upside down with His love and His grace. Let us say to our wonderful young people that the abundant rain of the Lord is on the way! Let us say to our precious nation that Satan is a liar for America is not done yet. There are men and women of God rising up in the coming generations that will tear the world up with the gospel of Jesus Christ. There is hope for them. There is a future for them. Their cloud is barely visible on the horizon even today!

> *1ˢᵗ Kings 18:41-45, "⁴¹ And Elijah said unto Ahab, Get thee up, eat and drink; for there is a sound of abundance of rain. ⁴² So Ahab went up to eat and to drink. And Elijah went up to the top of Carmel; and he cast himself down upon the earth, and put his face between his knees, ⁴³ And said to his servant, Go up now, look toward the sea. And he went up, and looked, and said, There is nothing. And he said, Go again seven times. ⁴⁴ And it came to pass at the seventh time, that he said, Behold, there ariseth a little cloud out of the sea, like a man's hand. And he said, Go*

up, say unto Ahab, Prepare thy chariot, and get thee down, that the rain stop thee not. [45] And it came to pass in the mean while, that the heaven was black with clouds and wind, and there was a great rain."

May the Lord of heaven and earth grant the abundant rain of His Presence to our children and to this nation that we love so much. Amen.

ABOUT THE AUTHOR

Jeanne S. Silvers is an ordained minister with over twenty years of hands-on experience in ministry. She obtained her Bachelor's Degree in Bible studies from the Jacksonville Theological Seminary in Jacksonville, Florida, while simultaneously working fulltime for the Department of the Navy and raising her children as a single mother.

Jeanne has worked alongside senior pastors and church leaders to see their own vision for the work of the Lord come to pass, and in so doing has acquired a deep and abiding respect for pastors and a thorough practical understanding of the workings of local congregations.

Her rural, earthy roots contribute greatly to her ability to communicate effectively with the everyday believer, while her education and experience resounds with church leaders and workers. The testimony of her personal life story bears witness to her special heart for those who are broken and bruised in our nation.

She celebrates life as an intercessor, a Bible teacher, and a prolific writer, but her greatest earthly delight comes in her role as mother, grandmother, and great-grandmother.

Readers can continue to enjoy her dialogue at www.someonetellthekids.blogspot.com.

NOTES

1   Romans 13:1
2   Robert Sparks Walker, *Torchlight to the Cherokees* [The Overmountain Press, 1993]
3   Psalm 1:3
4   2 Corinthians 1:22
5   Luke 24:49
6   Psalm 17:8
7   Buckminster Fuller, The Buckminster Fuller Institute, By permission
8   Matthew 5:16
9   1 Peter 2:9
10 Philip Paul Bliss. 1838. *Almost Persuaded*
11 2 Kings 1:8
12 1 Kings 18:29
13 1 Kings 18:17
14 Romans 12:2
15 *The Complete Word Study of the Old Testament,* Zodhiates
16 Helen Saul, *Phobias: Fighting the Fear* [Arcade Publishing, 2002]
17 Ibid.
18 Colossians 2:2
19 William Kethe, *All People that on Earth Do Dwell,* 1561
20 John Cennick and Charles Wesley, *Lo! He Comes,* 1752
21 Charles Wesley, *Depth of Mercy* ,1740
22 John Newston, *Amazing Grace,* 1779

23   Matthew Bridges and Godfrey Thring, *Crown Him with Many Crowns*, 1852-1874

24   Carrie E. Breck, *Face to Face*, 1898

25   Rowland Hill, *Holy Ghost, with Light Divine*, 1783

26   Thomas O. Chisholm, *Great Is Thy Faithfulness,* © 1923. Ren. 1951 Hope Publishing Co., Carol Stream, IL 60188, www. hopepublishing.com, All rights reserved. Used by permission

27   Psalm 45:1

28   1 Timothy 6:6

29   U. S. Bureau of the Census, 2010. "Median Age and Sex Composition in the United States, 2010," http://www.census.gov/population/age [accessed October 2013]

30   *Adam Clarke's Commentary on the Bible* [Baker Publishing Group, 1983]

31   Ibid.

32   *The Complete Word Study of the New Testament*, Zodhiates

33   Luke 2:11-12

34   2 Corinthians 11:14

35   Eugene H. Peterson, *The Message Bible*, 2005

36   Psalm 107:2

37   Bruce L. Shelley, *Church History in Plain Language.* 3rd ed. [Thomas Nelson Publishers, 2008]

38   Romans 10:17

39   Terry Mattingly, "Religion Losing Some Appeal," *Indianapolis Star*, October 9, 2012

40   National Institute of Mental Health. http://www.nimh.gov/health [accessed July 2013]

41   Hosea 8:7

42   Matthew 9:33

43   Genesis 1:26

44   Eric Metaxas, *Bonhoeffer, Pastor, Martyr, Prophet, Spy* [Thomas Nelson Publishers, 2010]

45   1 Kings 18:28

46   Numbers 12:10

47   Hebrews 5:1

48 John 6:70

49 Matthew 6:10

50 U. S. Bureau of Labor Statistics, 2012, "American Time Use Survey Summary," http://www.bls.gov/news.release/atus [accessed June 2012]

51 Judson W. Van DeVenter, Winfield S. Weeden, Donald P. Hustad, *I Surrender All*, 1918

52 *The Complete Word Study of the New Testament*, Zodhiates

53 Adelaide A. Pollard and George C. Stebbins, *Have Thine Own Way, Lord*, 1907

54 Charles A. Tindley and F. A. Clark, *Nothing Between*, 1905

55 W. O. Palmer and J. E. White, *The Gospel Primer*. 4th ed. [Review and Herald Publishing, 1894] 7

56 Ibid, 19

57 Ecclesiastes 1:9

58 Frances R. Havergal and Philip P. Bliss, *I Gave My Life for Thee*, 1858

59 Ephesians 4:15

60 Philippians 2:15

61 Homer A. Kent, Jr., *Jerusalem to Rome, Studies in Acts* [Baker Book House, 1988] 21

62 Romans 8:10

63 John 20:28

64 Acts 17:6

65 Hebrews 11:6

66 Matthew 14:31

67 Mark 9

68 Romans 8:31

69 Luke 12:32

70 Luke 19:11-27

71 Terry Mattingly, "Religion Losing Some Appeal," *Indianapolis Star*, October 9, 2012

72 Galatians 5:22-23

73 Romans 8:17

74 Hebrews 7:25

75 Acts 10:34

[76] Helen Saul, *Phobias: Fighting the Fears* [Arcade Publishing, 2002]
[77] Taro Gomi, *Everybody Poops* [Kane/Miller Book Publishers, 2012]
[78] Genesis 2:18
[79] Genesis 2:23
[80] Romans 3:10
[81] Genesis 1:26
[82] Luke 12
[83] 1 Kings 19:19
[84] Isaiah G. Martin, *The Eastern Gate,* 1905
[85] Matthew 24:42
[86] 1 Peter 4:18
[87] Mark 14:8
[88] *Full Life Study Bible*, Zondervan

BIBLIOGRAPHY

Clark, Adam, *Commentary on the Bible*. Baker Publishing Group, 1983.

Kent, Homer A., *Jerusalem to Rome, Studies in Acts*. Baker Book House, 1988.

Metaxas, Eric, *Bonhoeffer, Pastor, Martyr, Prophet, Spy*. Thomas Nelson Publishers, 2010.

Palmer, W. O. and J. E. White, *The Gospel Primer*. 4th ed. Review and Herald Publishing, 1894.

Peterson, Eugene H., *The Message Bible*, 2005.

Saul, Helen, *Phobias: Fighting the Fear*. Arcade Publishing, 2002.

Shelley, Bruce, *Church History in Plain Language*. 3rd ed. Thomas Nelson Publishers, 2008.

Walker, Robert Sparks, *Torchlight to the Cherokees*. The Overmountain Press, 1993.

Zodhiates, Spiros, *The Complete Word Study of the Old Testament*. World Bible Publishers, Inc., 1992

Zodhiates, Spiros, *The Complete Word Study of the New Testament*. World Bible Publishers, Inc., 1992

Zondervan, *Full Life Study Bible*. Zondervan Publishing House

Zondervan, *The Comparative Study Bible*. Zondervan Publishing House